For Children Ages 3-12

HERO
TRAINING CAMP

HERO
IN TRAINING

An activity-based biblical study of the conscience for kids. Use in the home, in groups, or as **VBS** or Family **VBS**.

By Dr. Scott Turansky and Joanne Miller, RN, BSN

Authors
Dr. Scott Turansky and
Joanne Miller, RN, BSN

Graphic Designer
Ellen Cranstoun

Illustrator
Ron Wheeler

Special thanks to Laura Rizkallah and her family for testing out this material and providing valuable feedback.

Published in Lawrenceville, NJ by the National Center for Biblical Parenting

National Center for Biblical Parenting is a nonprofit corporation committed to the communication of sound biblical parenting principles through teaching, counseling, and the publication of written, audio, and video materials.

First Printing, December 2009

For information regarding permission or to find other resources for the family, contact:

76 Hopatcong Drive, Lawrenceville, NJ 08648-4136
(800) 771-8334 or (609) 771-8002
Email: parent@biblicalparenting.org
Web: biblicalparenting.org

Legal Information

In the Hero Training Camp Materials, here's what you can and can't do when reproducing.

Hero Training Camp Children's Curriculum

This curriculum is not reproducible except for the activity pages and crafts at the end of each lesson. When using this curriculum for VBS or Family VBS, it is recommended that each Station Manager and the Director have a copy of the Hero Training Camp children's curriculum. You may purchase additional copies of Hero Training Camp at 40% off.

Hero Training Camp VBS Director's Manual

This manual is fully reproducible for use in your church, but is not reproducible to pass on to other churches.

Hero Training Camp VBS Preschool Coordinator's Manual

This manual is fully reproducible for use in your church, but is not reproducible to pass on to other churches.

Hero Training Camp Music CD

All the files on this CD including audio, visual, and sheet music are reproducible for your family or your church but it is not permitted to reproduce it for another church.

Hero Training Camp VBS and Family VBS Resource CDs

All the files on these CDs are fully reproducible for use in your church but are not reproducible to pass on to other churches.

Hero Training Camp Family VBS Leader's Guide

This manual is fully reproducible for use in your church, but is not reproducible to pass on to other churches.

Table of Contents

Biblical Basis for Hero Training Camp

Hero Training Camp is designed for use in a classroom or in the home. It's been created to teach children about the biblical concept of the conscience. The word "conscience" is used 30 times in the New Testament and is illustrated throughout the Bible many, many times, but most children rarely understand the importance of the conscience for their own lives. Studying the scriptures reveals that the conscience prompts people to seek God and salvation, and then also helps them live rightly each day. In particular the conscience prompts children in four ways: Do what's right, deal with wrongs, be honest, and care about others.

The conscience helps to make a hero, both in biblical times and today. Heroes are characterized by four things: They do what's right, deal with wrongs, are honest, and they care about others. Children can learn to be heroes right now in their homes, with their friends, and with others. As they practice being heroes in the small things, they will prepare their hearts for bigger opportunities to demonstrate heroism as well.

Throughout this curriculum children will learn about their own hearts. In particular they'll learn how to be internally motivated, prompted by the conscience and the Holy Spirit in their lives. If a child you're working with hasn't yet trusted Christ as his or her personal Lord and savior, you'll find a number of opportunities to talk about the benefits of that significant choice, one of them being the indwelling of the Holy Spirit in one's heart.

Each lesson in **Hero Training Camp** contains a story from the Old Testament and emphasizes a different part of David's life. The Bible stories provide many discussion points about what a hero is and how children can exemplify those same qualities in their lives right now.

As you teach this material, take time to pray for your children. Pray that God will change their hearts, give them a vision for being the people God has called them to be, and that you will have wisdom to know how to take advantage of the teachable moments provided by the activities, games, crafts, and even the snack time.

In this curriculum children will be challenged in a number of ways with the idea that they can be heroes now. That's how God designed them. That's what living for God is all about. It's our prayer that these lessons will give children a vision for living their lives for God. After all, that's what a true hero is.

Blessings,

Scott Turansky   *Joanne Miller*

How to Use Hero Training Camp

★ ★ ★ ★ ★

Hero Training Camp is designed for children ages 3-12 and engages kids through activity, the language of children. Through science experiments, music, games, Bible stories, craft projects, and snacks, kids learn more about what it means to be a hero in everyday life.

Hero Training Camp combines Bible stories from the life of David with the theological concept of the conscience to teach children in practical ways about God's desire to work in and through them in this world.

In Your Family

Hero Training Camp was designed for use in a home environment. In particular, as a parent, you'll want to pay attention to the Parent Power, Conscience Insight, Seeing it Through the Eyes of a Child, and Introduction to the lesson in order to glean thoughts and ideas for discussions with your children. You may want to invite friends or neighbor children to enjoy Hero Training Camp with you. If you have children that are older than twelve years old, you might have them help teach the material to the younger children. Older kids love the science experiments and planning the games and activities.

In a family environment it's usually best to break up each lesson over several sessions of training and fun, making the most of informal dialogue in between. For example, you might do one lesson a week but have five sessions of activity and training during that week. Repeat the theme and power words often, remind children of the Bible story for that lesson, and look for creative ways to raise the awareness level of being a hero in everyday life.

Although you don't need anything else, additional resources are available for family use if you'd like. You may want to purchase posters, shirts, hats, or the Hero Training Camp Music CD that contains both audio and video versions of the Hero Song and Conscience Song to build memories. Look at these and other resources at biblicalparenting.org/HeroInMyHome.asp.

In Your Church

Hero Training Camp can be used very effectively in Sunday School or Children's Church as a stand-alone curriculum. Or, you might consider using the parent training video series entitled "Everyday Parents CAN Raise Extraordinary Kids" so that parents are learning parenting strategies that complement what the children are learning.

Either way you'll want to plan ahead to photocopy the appropriate pages for that lesson and gather the craft supplies. All supplies needed are designed to be easily accessible but you might want to check just to make sure you have those things in stock. The beginning of each lesson gives you a convenient list to help you in preparation.

The sections entitled Parent Power and Conscience Insight were designed primarily for when the curriculum is used in the home by parents, so you might just read over those sections for your own benefit.

Although not required, support materials are provided for you if you want to enhance the Hero Training Camp experience for your church. You might want to purchase the Hero Training Camp Music CD that contains both audio and video of the two songs. Posters, fliers, shirts, and many other ideas are available at biblicalparenting.org/HeroInMyChurch.asp.

Hero Training Camp VBS

Hero Training Camp is designed for use as a stand-alone VBS program. The first five lessons provide just enough content for five sessions of Hero Training Camp VBS. You'll see a combination of high-energy activity, group discussion, and table time. You may disregard the last three sessions or use them as a special emphasis some other time during the year.

You'll want to purchase the Hero Training Camp VBS Kit that contains the Hero Training Camp Music CD, fliers, registration materials, and the VBS Leader's Guide to help you through the organizational and planning process.

Find out about all of the support materials such as shirts, banners, posters, fliers, and much more at biblicalparenting.org/HeroTrainingCampVBS.asp.

Hero Training Camp Family VBS Plus

Hero Training Camp Family VBS Plus is designed to meet the growing desire to bring families together for training and fun. Usually scheduled in the evenings, Hero Training Camp Family VBS contains five 90-minute sessions. Each evening parents and kids are together for 15 minutes in an interactive game or activity. Then parents and children separate for training on their own level for one hour. At the end of the evening, parents and children join again for a debriefing time.

The Hero Training Camp Family VBS Plus Curriculum contains the children's program and complementary video materials for parents entitled "Everyday Parents CAN Raise Extraordinary Kids."

You'll want to purchase the Family VBS Plus Kit that contains the extra activities and materials necessary. In addition, you may want to purchase posters, banners, fliers, shirts, and other support materials to enhance your Family VBS experience.

What does the "Plus" stand for? That's even more fun. After a week of Hero Training Camp Family VBS, as an option, your church can offer three more Family Night activities to bring families together in the coming months. One Friday or Saturday evening a month bring families together for Family Night and use the remaining three lessons to encourage further growth together. Wow. Now your VBS has taken on a whole new dimension.

Learn more about the support materials for Family VBS and Family Nights Hero Training Camp at biblicalparenting.org/FamilyVBSPlus.asp.

No matter how you use Hero Training Camp, you'll have a blast! Kids will have fun but most importantly you'll engage them in significant conversations about who they are, how God has made them, and how he wants to do a special work in and through them.

Special Hints and Tips

★ ★ ★ ★ ★

Hero Training Camp is about learning the skills to be heroes, but it's much more than that. Children will also learn about the importance of the conscience and the role of the Holy Spirit in their lives as they study the life of David. Here are some important thoughts to keep in mind as you teach these lessons to the children.

Length of Each Lesson

Each lesson is designed to be used in a variety of contexts. If you're using this material in a classroom you'll find that each lesson contains enough teaching and activities for 90-120 minutes of class time. If you're using this in your home, then you will likely want to spread each lesson over several days, maximizing the discussion and teaching points. If you need to shorten the time, you may want to leave out a few activities but be sure to use whatever ones you do teach to emphasize the theme for that lesson.

Age Appropriateness

The Hero Training Camp is for children ages 3-12. Because the developmental stages provide differing levels of comprehension, you'll want to tailor the program accordingly. In lessons where an activity exists for older children, an activity for younger children is also provided. Suggestions for working with preschoolers are included throughout the lessons since some of the concepts taught are abstract and may require some modification or simplification to appeal to the concrete thinking of a younger child. If you have children over the age of 12 you might want to have them help teach the curriculum to younger children. Many of the activities appeal to older children, and allowing them to teach the lessons gives them an ability to learn the material themselves.

Plan Ahead

Each lesson requires that you gather supplies or test out science experiments or craft projects in advance. A list of supplies is provided at the beginning of each lesson to make it clear what's needed

for that lesson. As you complete each session, take a look at the next lesson and its activities in order to gather what's needed. All activities require basic items that you might have around the house or classroom, but you'll need time to prepare and test them for yourself.

Equipping Parents

Parent letters are provided at the end of each lesson. If you're doing these lessons in your home, you'll want to read the letters yourself for hints of how to apply the material during the rest of the week. If you're doing the sessions in a classroom, be sure to copy enough letters for parents so that they can follow up with children at home. Each lesson contains a parenting tip called "Parent Power." If you're doing this curriculum as a family, you'll want to look at those tips to further develop the concept in the lesson.

Lesson Theme, Power Words, Theological Truth, and Bible Verse

Each session contains a Theme that you'll want to reinforce several times throughout the lesson. In fact, you might stop after every activity and ask, "What is the lesson we're trying to learn in this activity?" That lesson should somehow be tied to the theme for that session. The Power Words are designed for the child to say. Many times the things that kids say to themselves can mean all the difference between hero actions and those that are disruptive or unhelpful. The Theological Truth summarizes an important principle about God's design and is expressed in a personal way that a child can understand. Each lesson provides a Bible verse for children to memorize. Remember that God is the one who changes a person's heart and one of his tools to do that is the Bible. Take time to talk about the Bible verse for the day and encourage children to memorize it.

The conscience is an important concept and it's fun to watch children catch a glimpse of its value for their own lives. Because there are so many different practical benefits of the conscience, you'll want to take your time and amplify the lessons learned. It may be one activity or an illustration that helps them get it. Don't hesitate to camp out in places where children seem most responsive.

Songs

Songs have been created for Hero Training Camp. The first song, entitled The Hero Song, written by Alan Root and emphasizes the importance of the conscience and the Holy Spirit in a child's life and ties them both into the idea of being a hero. The second song is called The Conscience Song and is also sung by Alan Root. It warns children about temptation and talks about the voice of God reminding them to do the right thing. Both of these songs are available in audio and video format on the Hero Training Camp Music CD purchased separately.

Role Plays

Each lesson contains some kind of role play. The reality is that many children are good at parroting the right answers back. Role plays have the ability to help children work through the concepts a bit more. When kids have to act it out, it forces them to think creatively about the lesson and produce some real life solutions. It's amazing how often those solutions then will reveal themselves in life. Enjoy the role plays and recognize that they are a great tool to help move the truths from the head to the heart.

Hero Field Guide

The Hero Field Guide is a booklet containing the Bible verses and Power Words for each lesson. If you're using Hero Training Camp as a VBS program or Family VBS then you'll want to use the five-session version provided in those kits instead. The Hero Field Guide is an excellent tool to help children remember the lessons learned throughout the program.

Camera

Each lesson provides photo opportunities. These photos can be used for review, promotion, or simply to enjoy. Posting them on the web can allow others to see what you've done and what the children are learning. Keep the camera close at hand and use it regularly in each session. You might even assign a person to be the amateur photographer for Hero Training Camp.

Send Us Your Pictures

We, at the National Center for Biblical Parenting, are always interested in hearing your stories and seeing your pictures. Please take time to tell us how this material has helped you and the children you work with. Also send us pictures. We'd love to see your kids learning how to be heroes and developing their skills in Hero Training Camp.

I Can Be a HERO

Preparing Your Heart to Teach Session 1

God placed a conscience inside each person. The primary function of the conscience is to point people to a personal knowledge of God. Romans 2:15 describes the conscience as an internal witness inside non-believers that acknowledges God's existence.

The conscience has other tasks as well. When the apostle Paul stood before Felix, the governor, he defended his ministry by saying, "I strive always to keep my conscience clear before God and man" (Acts 24:16). Paul relied on his conscience for more than salvation. He used it in his daily life. He made another defense before the Sanhedrin in Acts 23:1 when he said, "I have fulfilled my duty to God in all good conscience to this day."

Paul considered the conscience so important that he mentions it 20 times in his epistles. Five of those times he tells Timothy, a young pastor, about the importance of a conscience and the danger of abandoning it. In 1 Timothy 1:18-19 he says, "fight the good fight, holding on to faith and a good conscience."

The apostle Peter also showed high regard for the conscience by mentioning it three times in his first epistle (2:19, 3:16, and 3:21). In 1 Peter 3:15-16 he says, "Always be prepared to give an answer to everyone who asks you to give the reason for the hope that you have. But do this with gentleness and respect, keeping a clear conscience, so that those who speak maliciously against your good behavior in Christ may be ashamed of their slander."

Many other passages in the New Testament and the Old Testament allude to the work of the conscience in a person's life. It's clearly an important internal motivator that points people to do right and deal with wrongs.

But how do you help a five-year-old or a ten-year-old catch a vision for the importance of the conscience? And greater yet, of what practical value is the conscience for children? Could it be that there is a way to work with children that takes the conscience into account? Hero Training Camp helps children and their parents understand how to practically apply the biblical concept of the conscience. In fact, tremendous benefits come to children who understand and take advantage of the blessing it provides. In particular, those children become internally motivated instead of always relying on parental promptings.

There's much more to learn about the conscience and much of it is revealed throughout this children's program. It is our goal to help teachers and parents also learn about their own consciences, so please take time to read the extra teaching notes that will help you understand the value of the conscience for you as well as the kids you're teaching.

For preschoolers: Neither the concept of the Holy Spirit nor the conscience are easily understood by young children. So to help preschoolers through this lesson you'll want to focus on words like "the heart," "God," and "doing what's right."

Session 1 ★ I Can Be a Hero

Supplies Needed for this Lesson

Hero Shield
Supplies needed: Photocopy the Hero Shield on page 25. Also provide crayons or markers.

Hero Training Creed
Supplies needed: Photocopy the Hero Training Creed from page 26 and mount it nicely on construction paper.

Floating Paper Clip
Supplies needed: Small paper clip, a bowl of water, and a paper towel

5 Cups – Which Voice?
Supplies needed: 5 cups, a few pieces of nice candy, slips of paper, your Bible, and a pen or pencil

Hero Skill Building Activity
Pass the Ball
Supplies needed: Three bath or beach towels and a ball. This ball could be a football or may need to be a softer ball if played indoors.

WHAT'S WRONG? Game
Supplies needed: One copy of each of the ten pictures at the end of this lesson and one copy of the Hero Search Sheet for each child. Mount the ten pictures around the room at eye level so that children can see them easily. Distribute the Hero Search Sheets so that each child has one. Provide a pen or pencil for each child.

Hero Field Guide
Supplies needed: Photocopy, fold, and staple (like a book) the pages at the end of this manual for the Hero Field Guide. If possible, duplicate the cover on construction paper or card stock. Also photocopy the verse for today on page 39, plus glue, and crayons or markers.

Hero Trophy
Supplies needed: Photocopy onto card stock the Hero Trophy page at the end of this lesson. One toilet paper roll per child, scissors, glue, and markers

Fruit Burrito
Supplies needed: Fresh small flour tortillas, cream cheese, cinnamon, raisins, apple, knife, paper plates, and plastic spoons or knives for spreading

Other suggested items:
- Photocopy the Parent Letter for each student.
- If you have the Hero Training Camp Music CD, be prepared to play the Hero Song in this lesson. You may purchase the Hero Training Camp Music CD at biblicalparenting.org.
- A camera to take pictures of the kids.

Theme
God has placed inside of you the ability to see problems and take action. Your job is to develop this awareness so that you can use it to be a hero.

Power Words
I am eager to do what's right.

Theological Truth
I have a conscience and God wants to use it to help me develop into a hero.

Welcome Activity
Hero Shield

Supplies needed: Photocopy the Hero Shield on page 25. Also provide crayons or markers.

Greet children with delight as they come to Hero Training Camp. Have them sit down and, using markers or crayons, decorate the four parts of the hero shield and write their name on the banner. This piece will later be used in the Hero Field Guide.

Together Time

I will LISTEN with my 👁 👁, keep my 👄 UNDER CONTROL, Do what the 👨 SAYS, knowing that becoming a HERO for God is MY GOAL.

Gather children together for some teaching. Start by introducing the Hero Training Creed. (Use the poster on page 26.) Repeat it as often as necessary in the classroom so that the children understand it. Refer to it when correcting children or guiding them to the next activity. In particular, explain listening with my eyes, since that's a play on words and may be confusing at first.

Hero Training Creed

I will listen with my eyes, keep my mouth under control, do what the teacher says, knowing that becoming a hero for God is my goal.

Introduction
Floating Paper Clip

Supplies needed: Small paper clip, a bowl of water, and a paper towel

Instructions: "When I drop this paper clip into the bowl do you think it will sink or float?" Go ahead and drop the paper clip into the bowl to demonstrate that it sinks. "Today I'm going to show you how you can make a paper clip float on top of the water." Take a piece of paper towel about one inch square and lay it gently on top of the water. Place the paper clip on top of the paper towel so that it rests carefully on top of the water. Then using another tool push the paper towel down so that it drops to the bottom leaving the paper clip floating on the water. It takes a bit of skill to

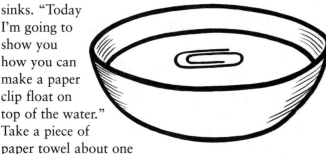

gently place the paper clip on the paper towel, so take your time and be ready to try it a few times before you're successful.

How it works: "Isn't that amazing that the paper clip is floating on top of the water? Let me tell you why that works. Water has a skin. We don't usually think about it that way but the edges of water create a boundary for it. You can also see this when I put several drops of water on the table. The water stays together instead of spreading out on the table because the "skin" of the water keeps it together. So when you put the paper clip on top of the water the skin of the water keeps the paper clip afloat."

Discussion points: Most people don't realize this about water even though water is around them every day. If you understand how it works, you can float a paper clip. You're going to learn some more things about life here in our Hero Training Camp. One of the most important things you're going to learn is that you have some things inside of you that maybe you never realized before. In fact, those are the things that help you to be a hero. You have them. We all do. But you must know what they are and how to use them. You need to know some important secrets. In this first lesson you will learn to pay attention to something inside you. It's already there. You just need to know what to do with it. Heroes do. They are aware of things going on right around them. We're going to teach you all about it while you're here with us in Hero Training Camp.

★ ★ ★ ★ ★

Bible Story
A Hero in the Making

This Bible story is taken from 1 Samuel 16. Use the Bible and the following thoughts to teach the story and the lesson to the children. You may have to change the wording to match the developmental level of the children you're working with.

David was the youngest boy in his family. He had seven older brothers. His job was to take care of the sheep. He also loved music. He played an instrument called a lyre. That's like a harp or even like a guitar. He loved to write songs while he was out in the fields watching his sheep. A lot of his songs were about God and about his relationship with him. One song imagined God being a shepherd just like him. David thought, "If God were a shepherd then I'd like to be one of his sheep." Maybe some of you know this psalm. It's Psalm 23 and reads this way:

The LORD is my shepherd, I lack nothing. He makes me lie down in green pastures, he leads me beside quiet waters, he refreshes my soul. He guides me along the right paths for his name's sake. Even though I walk through the darkest valley, I will fear no evil, for you are with me; your rod and your staff, they comfort me. You prepare a table before me in the presence of my enemies. You anoint my head with oil; my cup overflows. Surely your goodness and love will follow me all the days of my life, and I will dwell in the house of the LORD forever.

David had a special relationship with God. David also had some important things going on in his heart. He wanted to do what's right. He only had a small job to do now and that was to take care of sheep. But he did that job well. And people were already beginning to notice – and God was watching.

Now it just so happened that about that time, God was looking for someone to help him solve a problem. The present king of Israel wasn't obeying him. God needed a new king and his servant, the prophet Samuel, would be used to find him. God sent Samuel to Bethlehem, David's hometown. The people all wondered why this great man was coming to their small town. In fact, they were afraid and wondered if they had done something wrong. No, Samuel's visit wasn't because the people had done anything wrong. It was because God wanted to choose a new king and that new king would come from Bethlehem and from the home of Jesse.

"Jesse! Wow, that's my dad," David thought. "What a privilege. To have the king from my own family."

A servant from the house came running out to find David in the field. "Samuel is in the house and he's looked at all of your brothers to see which one will be the next king. But Samuel didn't see the one God wanted. So they sent me out to get you and bring you back to the house."

When David walked into the house Samuel knew that he was the one. David would be the next king of Israel. Of course, it wouldn't happen quite yet. After all, David was just a boy, but now David knew something very important. He would be the next king. Oh, David already knew that he had an important relationship with God. God had protected him when he was out at night with the sheep. God gave him several songs that reflected on God's power and majesty. But this was different. God had chosen him for a special task. The job of being the king. The job of being a hero.

God likes to do that. He often uses someone who is doing a good job with a little, and then gives that person a big job to do. David did a good job taking care of sheep and practicing his lyre and God could tell that he would make a good leader someday.

David had some good things going on in his heart already. You can also develop those things. Let's talk about this awareness you must develop in order to be a hero.

I want you to imagine being a shepherd for a moment. Tell me some things that would make you feel uncomfortable if you were in charge of the sheep. When I say uncomfortable I mean that feeling inside that something is wrong or that you need to be thinking about something. Sometimes people call it being responsible. What are some things that David would have to be thinking about all the time and, at times, make him feel uncomfortable? It's getting close to feeding time. I see a storm coming. That lamb is limping. Another lamb is wandering away. The sheep look thirsty. I wonder if there are any wolves around. All of those things would make David feel uncomfortable at times.

When do you think David could feel comfortable? Sure, when everything seems to be going well, the sheep are fed, watered, protected, and happy.

That feeling of being comfortable and uncomfortable was important to God. You see God can work more easily in a person's heart when that person is responsible and thoughtful about what's going on around him. In fact, God placed something inside all of our hearts called a conscience to help us feel comfortable or uncomfortable at times. We are going to learn more about the conscience in Hero Training Camp.

Of course, there was one problem. Israel already had a king. It would take many years before David would actually sit on the throne of Israel. That was okay though. He had plenty of work to do. David needed some training in his heart to do this great work. Eventually David would be one of the greatest heroes in Israel's history. But now, he needed some training, and life would provide that training. So back to the sheep for David. More songs. More listening to God. More being faithful

as a shepherd. More practice at doing what's right and learning to face challenges every day. David would learn to be a great hero in life by practicing on the small stuff every day.

God wants to do the same thing in your life. He has plans to make you a hero but it takes some work to get there. In fact, God uses the small things in your life right now to develop the hero inside of you.

One of the things God has done for you is that he gave you a conscience. The conscience is an important tool for becoming a hero. The first thing we have to do is become aware that it's there. We'll be practicing some skills today and working on some activities that will help you understand more about what your conscience is and how God wants to use it in your life in some exciting ways.

Take away: I have a conscience and God wants to use it to help me develop into a hero.

For preschoolers: Emphasize the importance of doing what's right every day, even when it seems small. God uses the small opportunities every day to prepare you for bigger things as you grow older.

Bible Verse
Romans 8:37
In all these things we are more than conquerors through him who loved us.

Game
5 Cups – Which Voice?

Supplies needed: 5 cups, a few pieces of nice candy, slips of paper, your Bible, and a pen or pencil

Before the activity begins, number each of the cups from one to five. Put one piece of candy under one of the cups. Prepare enough pieces of paper so that each child can have one. Put a number from one to five on each of the pieces of paper, except two or three pieces that should have something else written on them like "top desk drawer," or "in the tissue box."

Session 1 ★ I Can Be a Hero

Explain the rules of the game to the children this way. "As we learn about the conscience we also learn that God speaks to us. Sometimes he speaks about what's right and what's wrong.

"Sometimes God just reminds us that he loves us. In this activity I have a special candy hidden. (Point to the five cups on the table.) I will choose one person to be my listener. You don't know where it is, but if you choose the right place I will give you the candy. You could guess and maybe you'd be right, but you can be certain that you're right if you listen to the right person. At least one of the kids in this room is right."

Give slips of paper to each person in the room (except the listener) making sure that you know at least one child who has the right answer. "All of you with slips of paper may not know if you're right or not but your job is to persuade our listener to choose the location on your piece of paper. Persuaders, yell out to the listener which choice he should make. Do your best at persuading our listener to make the choice that's on your piece of paper."

As the teacher, you know which persuader has the right answer. Write on a piece of paper the name of that person, for example, "Listen to Carla." Place that piece of paper in your Bible.

Say "Go" and watch the persuaders try to convince the listener which cup to choose. After a few moments say, "Stop for a moment" and then say to the listener, "It sounds like you're getting a lot of advice. I have a clue that can help you. It's in my Bible." Hand the listener the clue and then say, "OK persuaders, you're going to have to work harder now since he has this clue. Ready, go." This time, as the persuaders do their work, the listener will be trying to find out what one particular person is saying. Then he can guess. When he guesses right give him the candy. Affirm those active persuaders, even those who were wrong, to

encourage them to actively persuade the next time.

Repeat the same activity. To hide the candy have all children put their heads between their knees facing down on the floor and make a swishing sound with their mouths, giving you just a moment to hide the candy again. Then collect and redistribute the papers. Take note of at least one child who gets the right one and write the clue on a paper again and put it in your Bible. Have the persuaders do their work and then give the clue again.

Repeat the activity a few times but the last time have the candy placed in one of the odd places like the top drawer of the desk or the box of tissues. In the past these were just thought to be irrelevant distractions but this time that location is the correct one.

Discussion points: After you've played the game several times ask the children, "What do you think was written on the paper in my Bible?" Children often think you wrote the answer or the number of the right cup. "No, I wrote the name of a person to listen to. Why do you think I did that?"

There are two important things going on inside of you. One is the conscience and the other is God's voice. Unfortunately there are other things speaking to us as well like friends and even our own desires and ideas. It's important to learn to pay attention to the right things in order to get the right answers for decisions we make every day in life. Heroes know how to pay attention like that.

I put the clue in the Bible because I want to remind us that God has answers in his Word for us. In fact, here's an interesting quote from Proverbs 4:1-4.

> Listen, my sons, to a father's instruction;
> pay attention and gain understanding. I give
> you sound learning, so do not forsake my
> teaching. For I too was a son to my father,
> still tender, and cherished by my mother.
> Then he taught me, and he said to me,
> "Take hold of my words with all your heart;
> keep my commands, and you will live."

One of the ways God helps you to develop inside, both the ability to listen to him and to pay attention to your conscience, is to listen to parents. That sure is interesting, isn't it? We don't just listen to parents to get the room cleaned or the homework done. We listen to parents because they have the clues to life. If you practice listening to the right person and if you read the Bible and pay attention to your conscience, you will be strengthening your ability to know what's right.

For preschoolers: Simplify this game by first allowing a child to guess which cup has the candy. Allow different children to guess, some may be right, others will be wrong. Then call one child over to you and tell the child you have a secret. You want to give him a hint. Whisper to the child the right answer, then allow the child to guess.

The point is that when we listen to the right voice, then we know what the right thing is to do. Remind children that God often speaks to children today to help them know the right thing to do. Sometimes that happens in their hearts and sometimes it happens through their parents.

What are some examples of things that parents say to children so they can do the right thing in life?

★ ★ ★ ★ ★

Role Play

Note: Have someone take pictures of the kids doing the role play and use them later for review and to share with others.

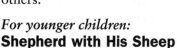

For younger children:
Shepherd with His Sheep

Choose one child to be David the shepherd, another to be a bear, and have the rest of the children act like sheep. Guide children through the

following role play by reading the statements and then allowing them to act out each part.

David was a shepherd boy. His job was to take care of all the sheep. (Go ahead shepherd, take care of some sheep.)

The sheep loved David. (Show how you love David.) Sometimes they were hungry, or thirsty (what does that look like?) and sometimes they would stray away or even be afraid that a bear was coming.

David's job was to think about the sheep all the time, to encourage them, rescue, feed, provide water, and protect them.

David had a sling. When he swung the sling round and round he could let it go and it would be like a weapon.

One day a bear came nearby. (Listen to the bear growl.) All the sheep were afraid. David swung his sling and ran toward the bear and the bear ran away.

David was careful to do the right thing. Sheep need to do the right thing too so that they can be protected.

(If you have time, you might play the role play again allowing different children to be the bear and David.)

For older children:
A Hero in the Making

Since drama is moved by emotion, take some time and prepare children for the role play by asking these questions and exploring their answers:

How would you feel if you were David and were the one that was picked instead of your brothers?

How would you feel if you were the older brothers and young David was chosen?

How would you feel if you were Samuel, the one having to pick just one boy?

Choose someone to be Samuel, the servant, and then choose several children to be Jesse, Jesse's wife, and Jesse's boys. (Allow girls to play the boys too.) Encourage children to act out the story as you read the following:

Samuel was given an assignment to go and find a king in Bethlehem at the home of Jesse. But God hadn't yet told him which boy would be the new king.

When Samuel came to Bethlehem he met Jesse and his family. (Everybody greet Samuel.)

As Samuel waited for God to tell him which boy would be king, Samuel looked at how nice looking all the boys were. (Go ahead Samuel, tell us what you're thinking about how nice everyone looks.)

God told Samuel that the boy he wanted had the right heart, but he wasn't in the room. So they sent the servant to go get David.

When David came into the room this is what happened:

Allow the students to take it from here, Samuel is excited, pleased with David, and says, "Yes, this is the one." The brothers and parents then have to react. Encourage some kids to respond very well and for the parents to respond well. Some children may feel jealous too.

At the end of the dialogue have everyone sit down and ask, "Do you think that was how the whole thing went?" "How might it have been different?"

Discussion points: Why do you think God chose David to be the next king? We know that David was used to doing the right thing. He knew how to take care of sheep and God knew that he would be a good one to take care of the people of Israel.

What kinds of things do you do well? At school? At home? With your parents? With your brothers and sisters? Around the house? In your bedroom? Heroes are made in the small stuff. So think about ways you can do what's right now.

★ ★ ★ ★ ★

Hero Skill Building Activity
Pass the Ball

Supplies needed: Three bath or beach towels and a ball. This ball could be a football or may need to be a softer ball if played indoors.

Instructions: Choose six children and have them pair up. Each pair of children holds one towel between them, one child at each end of the towel. Have the three pairs form a triangle. Hold up the ball and tell the children that the ball is very important and that their goal is to protect the ball from touching the ground. Put the ball into one of the towels and have the pair toss the ball by pulling the towel tight. The goal is to get the ball to another pair safely. The second pair passes to the third pair who then pass back to the first pair and so on. After passing the ball around twice to all three pairs, have the pairs step back two steps and try again. After going around two more times, have those children sit down and choose three more pairs. You may want to vary the distance between the pairs based on the age of the children. Remember that the goal is not to get them to drop the ball, but simply to be challenged as they protect it.

Discussion points: The goal of this activity was to protect the ball from hitting the ground while it was being passed around. Each one of us has a conscience that needs to be protected. You can damage your conscience by doing the wrong thing and trying to hide it, or by developing a pattern of lying. Sometimes people do the wrong thing so many times that they don't even care about it anymore. That causes damage to their consciences. It's very sad. One of the ways you can protect your conscience is by doing what you know to be right and correct wrongs when you make a mistake.

The conscience is an important treasure in a person's life. Your job is to protect it. It's one of the skills that makes a hero.

For preschoolers: Talk to children about doing the right thing. How does it feel when you do the right thing? It feels good. What are some things you can do to help out at home? How do you feel when you are a helper?

Conscience Insight

The conscience and the Holy Spirit both provide inner prompting for a child. They are not the same thing. The conscience prompts a child to do right or avoid doing wrong. The Holy Spirit may do that too but the Holy Spirit also empowers a person to do what's right. The conscience communicates its promptings through feelings. The Holy Spirit actually speaks to a person's heart. The conscience is a piece of equipment in a person's heart. The Holy Spirit is a person who wants to have a personal relationship with your child.

Hebrews 9:9 and 14 point out that it's salvation that cleanses the conscience. Furthermore, when a child relies on the Holy Spirit for control, the conscience is greatly empowered.

Regularly take time to talk to your child about spiritual things. Without salvation, the Holy Spirit, and the scriptures, a conscience simply seeks the highest good

that it knows, often proving inadequate as a tool.

But you can't simply ignore the conscience until a child becomes a Spirit-controlled believer. Training takes place now that provides a structure that God will eventually breathe life into.

One of the greatest things you can do for a child is to help him strengthen the conscience. As you do, it will become more and more powerful as a pointer to God himself.

The Hero Song

If you have the Hero Training Camp Music CD this is a good place to introduce the Hero Song.

Supplies needed: Hero Training Camp Music CD

Instructions: Play the Hero Song and ask children "What is this song trying to teach us?"

Discussion points: The conscience and the Holy Spirit help you choose what's right and avoid wrong.

Game

The WHAT'S WRONG? Game

Supplies needed: One copy of each of the ten pictures at the end of this lesson and one copy of the Hero Search Sheet for each child. Mount the ten pictures around the room at eye level so that children can see them easily. Distribute the Hero Search Sheets so that each child has one. Provide a pen or pencil for each child.

Instructions: Give the children the following instructions. Heroes have the ability to see problems. They can tell when someone is hurt or something bad is happening. This next exercise is important for you in helping you to become a hero because it tests you to see if you can find out what's wrong. We have ten pictures hanging around the room. You have a Hero Search Sheet in your hand. Your goal is to find the picture that matches the statement on the search sheet. Write the picture's number on the line next to the hero solution. (Answers: 3, 10, 5, 1, 7, 4, 8, 6, 9, 2)

Discussion points: Was it hard or easy to find things that were wrong in the pictures? Is it easier to see the problem or is it easier to solve the problem? Heroes are on the lookout for problems to solve. They see things that are wrong and fix them. The fact that you can see problems in these pictures means that you have part of what it takes to be a hero.

For preschoolers: Because younger children can't read, you might hold the pictures up one at a time and ask the children, "What's wrong in this picture?" and "What might you do to make it right?"

Hero Field Guide

Supplies needed:
Photocopy, fold, and staple (like a book) the pages at the end of this manual for the Hero Field Guide. If possible, duplicate the cover on construction paper or card stock. Also photocopy the verse for today on page 39, plus glue, and crayons or markers.

Instructions: Give each child a copy of the Hero Field Guide booklet. Have the children glue onto the cover the hero shield that they worked on during the welcome time. The child's name should be neatly printed on the banner at the bottom of the hero shield. Have the children glue today's Bible verse onto the correct page, covering the words Session 1. Allow them time to color and decorate the page. Don't have the children take the booklets home but instead keep them until the end of Hero Training Camp so that each session children can add the new Bible verse.

Discussion points: On the front of the Hero Field Guide are four traffic signs. Use them to talk about the four parts of the conscience. Lead a discussion about the four parts: Do what's right (One way), deal with wrongs (Wrong way), be honest (street signs), care about others (Yield). Discuss with children why that road sign was chosen for that particular part of the conscience.

The verse for today is a quote from Paul the apostle. He knew that God helps people to overcome problems.

Before you leave this activity, read the whole page to the kids. Then collect the Field Guides and keep them for the next lesson.

For preschoolers: Although young children can't read, this guide contains scripture and power words that parents can use at home to reinforce the lessons. Or, you may want to use the Hero Color Sheet from page 38 instead.

The conscience provides internal prompters to children but many parents miss opportunities to strengthen these prompters. Instead, parents emphasize parental prompters. One of the ways to increase the strength of those internal prompters is to send children on missions where they have to rely on internal prompters and then take initiative themselves. Instead of saying, "Billy, go clean up the Legos in the playroom," you might say, "Billy, would you please go look in the playroom and see if you can see anything out of place in there?" Teaching children to see what needs to be done is the first step toward motivating them to make changes on their own. You might also say, "Oops, Billy, think for a minute," as he's about to leave the table without clearing his space. Or, "Jim, would you please think of a way you can help in these frustrating few minutes before dinner?" Raising the awareness often requires that parents allow children to fill in some of the blanks by seeing what needs to be done for themselves and then taking initiative to do it.

★ ★ ★ ★ ★

Craft
Hero Trophy

Supplies needed: Photocopy onto card stock the Hero Trophy page at the end of this lesson. One toilet paper roll per child, scissors, glue, and markers

Instructions: Today we're going to create a hero trophy. Trophies remind us of winning and heroes like to win. You will be able to take this trophy home and put it somewhere to remind you that you are learning how to win at life. (Allow children to choose the male or female hero.)

Take a few minutes and nicely color the hero. Then, cut out the hero and glue it to the toilet paper roll.

Discussion points: As children are working, talk about heroes with these kinds of questions:

Heroes look   for problems. What kinds of problems can they see?

Sometimes heroes have special powers. Can you think of a special power that a hero might have?

Some heroes turn bad. They use their powers for evil. Why do you think that is?

Why do you think some kids try to be like the villain instead of a hero?

Why is it important to do what's right?

When heroes do the right thing, how do you think they usually feel?

The point of the discussion is that some kids don't want to be heroes. They try to use their powers to be mean or disrespectful or defiant. That person feels sad on the inside. Only when someone responds to the conscience and to God can they enjoy the benefits of being a hero.

What are some ways that you can practice being a hero in your home?

Take pictures of children with their trophies.

★ ★ ★ ★ ★

Snack
Fruit Burrito

Supplies needed: Fresh small flour tortillas, cream cheese, cinnamon, raisins, apple, knife, paper plates, and plastic spoons or knives for spreading

Instructions: Give each child a paper plate and a tortilla. Have children spread some cream cheese over the tortilla and then add pieces of cut apple and raisins. Sprinkle on a little cinnamon if desired. Roll it up and eat it.

Discussion points: How many of you like Mexican food? Sometimes it's spicy but not always. Today we're going to make a fun fruity burrito. You've probably never had something like this. It tastes delicious and it's fun to make.

In fact, a fruit burrito is a new idea. Heroes are creative and often think of new ways to approach common problems in life.

★ ★ ★ ★ ★

HERO Exercise

As you practice at home, be on the lookout for things that are wrong and see what you can do to fix them. Be ready to report back the next time we meet. Always remember to be careful who you listen to.

Conclusion

Who can identify something in this room that has a purpose and tell me what it is used for. Like the door knob on the door is used to open it. What else can you see? light on the ceiling, trash can, etc. Today we began to talk about something that is useful called the conscience.

Of course, the conscience isn't very useful until it is trained. God placed a conscience inside of you to help you sense what needs to be done. Just like a hero you have that ability on the inside. We did some activities today that illustrated important points about the conscience. We learned to see things that are wrong and talked about what we can do to fix problems we see. God has given you a conscience and the Holy Spirit to help you be aware of what needs to be done in life.

We learned about David who was just a shepherd boy when he was called to be a king, but God chose him to do great things.

God trains heroes in the small stuff. Today I'm going to give you a mission. This mission is to start practicing hero-like things. That means you look for problems in your family and you solve them. Maybe like some of the pictures we looked at in the game we played. You're a hero in training. You're looking to solve problems, not because you're going to get a reward, but because you like that good feeling inside when you do what's right and help others.

SEEING IT THROUGH THE EYES OF A CHILD

Mom: Bob, why is it that you don't leave your skates out when it's going to rain but you can't remember to take your bowl out of the living room and put it in the kitchen?

Bob: I don't know. I never thought about it. I guess... maybe... it's because I don't want to see my skates get damaged. They're valuable.

Mom: That's interesting. A clean house is valuable to me. But when you don't help me keep things clean, it makes me feel like you don't value me and what I want.

Bob: Oh Mom. I value you. I love you.

Mom: Do you think you could help me feel valued by cleaning up when you see something out of place?

Bob: OK, I'll try.

Mom: Thanks.

Prayer

Dear God, thank you for allowing us to learn to be heroes. Thank you for giving each of us a conscience and the Holy Spirit in our lives. Lord, would you please help us to see things that are out of place or missing or need to be done. Also, please give us the courage to do the right thing. Amen.

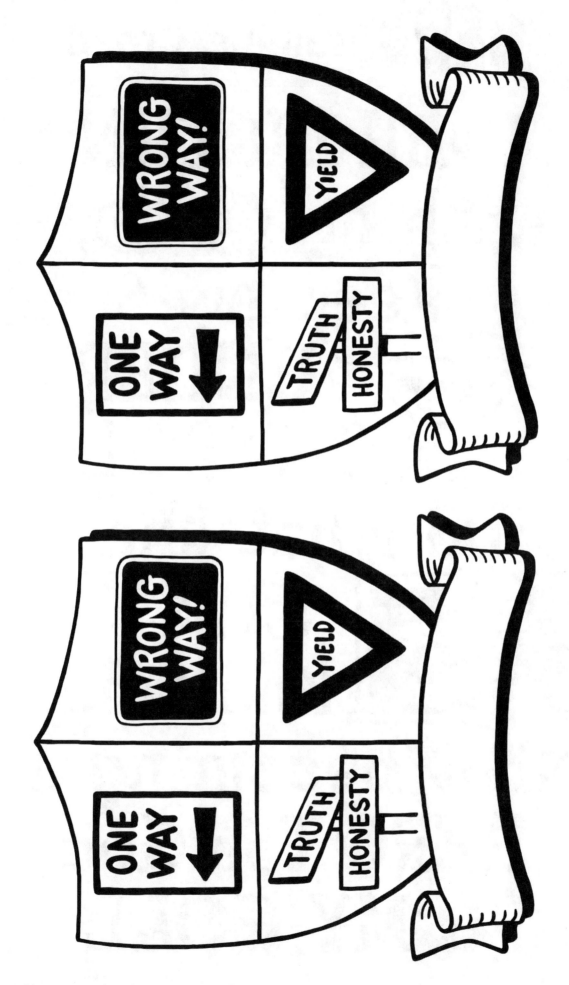

HERO Training Creed

I will LISTEN
with my 👁️👁️,
keep my 👄
UNDER
CONTROL,
Do what the
SAYS,
knowing
that becoming a
HERO for God
is MY GOAL.

Search Sheet

____ That girl is sad. Maybe I can invite her to join us.

____ That woman needs help with the door. I can help her.

____ I'll turn around at the bathroom door and see if I forgot anything.

____ I can help by taking out the trash.

____ Keeping myself under control is important for me and for others.

____ My mom has a lot to carry. Maybe I can help her.

____ I'll obey the signs. They are there to protect me.

____ When I come home I'll put my things away in the right places.

____ I can help clean up after dinner.

____ I could share with my friend.

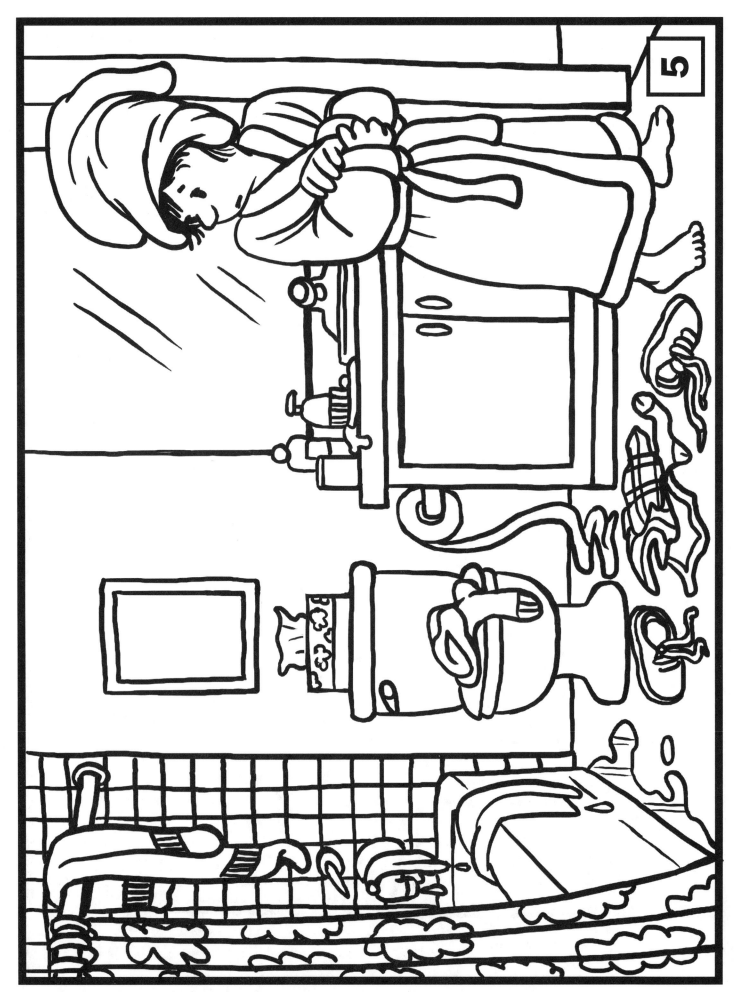

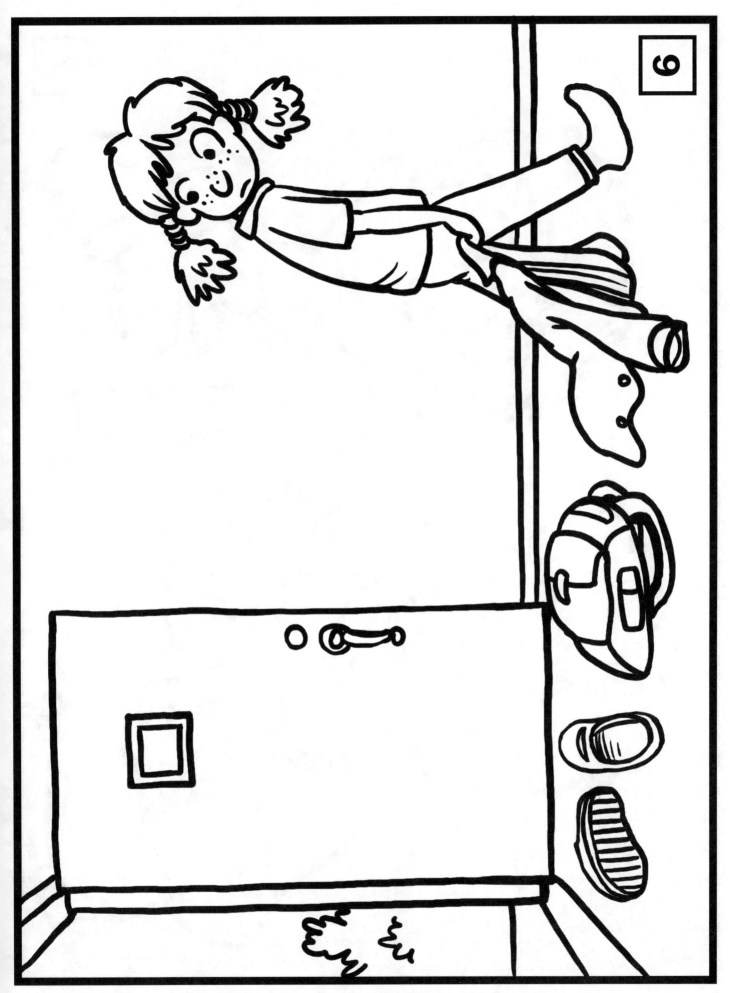

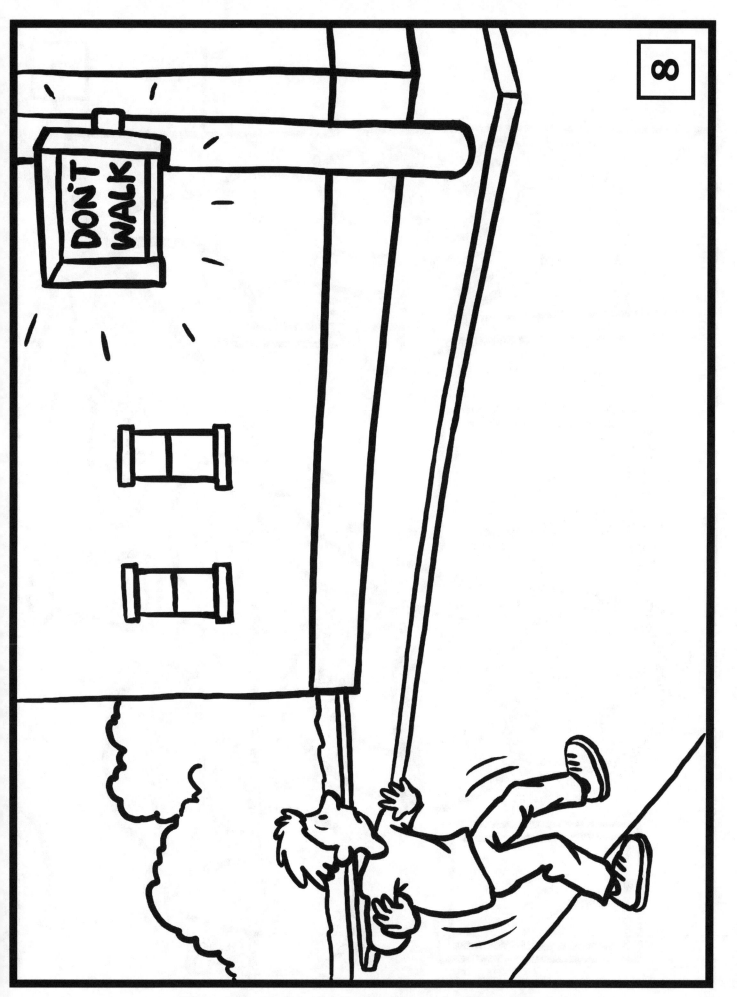

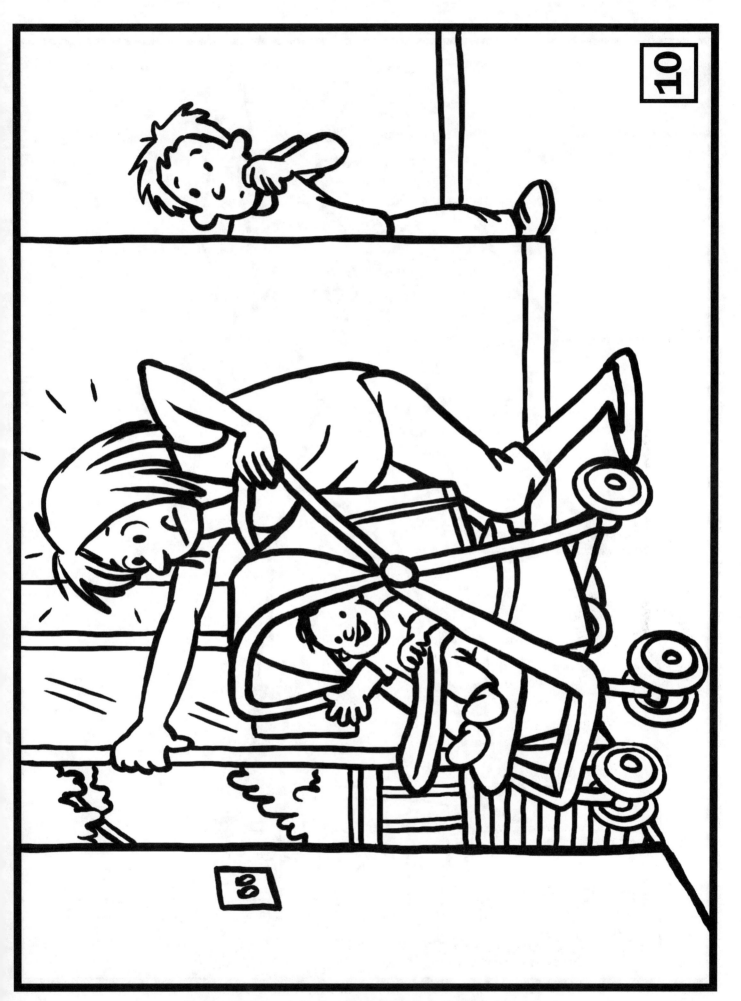

HEROES
DO WHAT'S RIGHT

In all these things
we are more than
conquerors
through him who
loved us.

Romans 8:37

In all these things
we are more than
conquerors
through him who
loved us.

Romans 8:37

In all these things
we are more than
conquerors
through him who
loved us.

Romans 8:37

In all these things
we are more than
conquerors
through him who
loved us.

Romans 8:37

HERO
Trophy

NATIONAL CENTER for BIBLICAL Parenting

76 Hopatcong Drive, Lawrenceville, NJ 08648-4136
(800) 771-8334 or (609) 771-8002
Email: parent@biblicalparenting.org
Web: biblicalparenting.org

Welcome to Hero Training Camp

Dear Parent,

The **Hero Training Camp** is designed to help children learn to be inner motivated in four ways: 1) Do what's right, 2) Deal with wrongs, 3) Be honest, 4) Care about others. The lessons teach children about two entities described in the Bible that provide motivation on the inside, the conscience and the Holy Spirit. God uses both to prompt children to take action.

The word "conscience" is used 30 times in the New Testament and is also alluded to both in the New and Old Testaments many other times. The Apostle Paul wrote in 1 Timothy 1:18-19, "fight the good fight, holding on to faith and a good conscience." Over and over again the conscience is mentioned as an important consideration.

The reason we call it **Hero Training Camp** is because heroes are characterized by the same four things. They do what's right, deal with wrongs, are honest, and care about others. At least, that's what a hero is supposed to do. Today sometimes the "good guy" is glorified even though he lacks one or more of those qualities. Furthermore, some children want to be like the bad guy instead of the good guy. **Hero Training Camp** provides opportunities to discuss these and many more issues.

The **Bible verse** for this lesson comes from Romans 8:37 and says, "In all these things we are more than conquerors through him who loved us." Look for opportunities to talk about what a clear conscience is and why it is so valuable.

The **Power Words** for this lesson are, "I am eager to do what's right." Children were given a **Hero Exercise** for this lesson to be on the lookout for things that are wrong and see what they can do to fix them. These might be common things around the house such as clothes on the floor, trash that needs to be emptied, a sad sibling, or someone who needs help. As you have opportunity, talk about things you see that need to change and encourage your child to do the same.

As you work with your child this week have some talks about heroes, how they see things that are out of place and take initiative to make things right. Talk about wanting to be like a hero and how some heroes are flawed.

The goal of this lesson is to raise the awareness level of three things. First, that the child has a conscience that points out problems and prompts action. Second, that God desires that your child learn to respond to the conscience and the Holy Spirit. And third, that when a child learns to respond well, hero opportunities arise. Your child can become a hero. Your home is the training ground. You are the coach. Welcome to **Hero Training Camp**.

Blessings,

Scott Turansky

Joanne Miller

Understanding the Mission

Preparing Your Heart to Teach Session 2

Growth is a process. Many children don't realize that fact. Lessons can be learned every day and those lessons become the valuable stepping stones for handling bigger and bigger challenges more successfully. In our story this week David fights the giant Goliath, but a closer look reveals that he had already fought some significant enemies in preparation for this larger battle.

Sometimes the lessons learned come from successfully mastering a particular problem. Other times, those lessons come from making a mistake. The important thing is to continue to learn and grow.

The conscience is a God-given tool but it is tainted by sin and therefore is unreliable on its own to be a guide for right behavior. 1 Corinthians 4:4 gives some interesting insights into the conscience. It says, "My conscience is clear, but that does not make me innocent." Simply stated, the conscience needs to be trained. It doesn't determine what right or wrong is. It just prompts a person to do right or avoid wrong. It must be tied to the external standard of the scriptures to be most effective.

This lesson helps children view current struggles and challenges as opportunities for growth instead of examples of inadequacy or failure. When children go home they will be challenged to look at problems or interruptions as opportunities to respond well, recognizing that the current struggles are preparation for the future.

Angry reactions are a common problem children face. Instead of reacting with anger, children must learn to face challenges with self-control. But that takes time to develop. In the same way that David responded well to challenges and was thus prepared to face the giant, children can practice positive responses to life now. Kids need strategies for addressing the things that provoke their anger. It's an internal adjustment that's needed and this lesson will give you opportunity to discuss anger

with the children. The next lesson will further develop the danger of relying on emotion to make decisions, giving children a greater ability to understand their own hearts.

Using the material in this lesson you'll be able to provide several examples of children who respond heroically now in the little challenges of life. With practice, these small heroic responses can build good patterns that God can use in more significant areas of life later on. If you want to be used by God to be a hero, then it starts right now.

Supplies Needed for this Lesson

Big Keys and the Little Paper Clip
Supplies needed: Key ring with two keys on it (not too heavy), string about three feet long, and a large paper clip

Potato Race
Supplies needed: Spoons, potatoes, bowls, and a camera

The Anger Bomb Game
Supplies needed: Photocopy for each child the two game pages from the end of this lesson (pages 54 and 55). Also provide paper lunch bags in which to take the game home.

Session 2 ★ Understanding the Mission

Hero Field Guide
Supplies needed: The Hero Field Guides made in the previous lesson. Also photocopy the verse for today on page 57, plus glue, and crayons or markers.

A Sling Shot
Supplies needed: Knee-high stockings (one stocking for each child), sand, plastic sandwich bags, rubber bands (2 per child), permanent felt pen, and scissors

David's Five Stones
Supplies needed: Honey Nut Cheerios, bananas, a knife, and a ziplock bag for each child

Other suggested items:
- Photocopy the Parent Letter for each student.
- Have a camera ready to take pictures.
- Be prepared to play the Hero Song if you have the Hero Training Camp Music CD.

Theme

Difficulties in life make heroes stronger to prepare them for handling bigger challenges that may come their way.

Power Words

Problems, interruptions, and challenges are my mission.

Theological Truth

I face challenges every day and, if I learn from them, I'll be able to handle bigger challenges later on in life.

Welcome Activity
Preparing the Bomb Game

Supplies needed: Copies of pages 54 and 55, scissors, Hero Song (optional)

Instructions: As children arrive have them neatly cut out the bombs for the game that will be played later. They can also cut out the fuses if there is

time. Give children the brown paper bags. Have them put their names on the bags and put the time bomb pieces inside.

If you have the Hero Training Camp Music CD play the Hero Song as children come into the room as a reminder that children are attending Hero Training Camp.

Together Time

I will LISTEN with my 👀, keep my 👄 UNDER CONTROL, Do what the 🧑‍🏫 SAYS, knowing that becoming a HERO for God is MY GOAL.

Gather together and remind children of the Hero Training Creed. Take a few moments to help children calm down and prepare their hearts with a prayer, asking God to settle their hearts and provide opportunity to focus on today's training.

Review the Hero Exercise that the children were assigned in the previous lesson. In our last lesson we looked for things that were wrong in life. Did any of you find things out of place or that needed some help?

Hero Training Creed:
> I will listen with my eyes, keep my mouth under control, do what the teacher says, knowing that becoming a hero for God is my goal.

Introduction
Big Keys and the Little Paper Clip

Supplies needed: Key ring with two keys on it (not too heavy), string about three feet long, and a large paper clip

Instructions: Tie the ring of keys to one end of the string and the paper clip to the other. Put the string over your finger and pull the paper clip down and up so that the keys move up and down as well. Ask the children, "What will happen if I let go of the paper clip?" The children should expect the keys to fall to the ground. You might even demonstrate that what they believe to be true actually does happen. Go ahead and let go of the paper clip and watch the keys fall to the ground.

"I'm going to show you a trick now that will use the paper clip to prevent the keys from hitting the ground. The reason I want to show you this is because the difference between being a hero and not being a hero is often a small thing. It just takes a little change for someone to learn to be a hero and that's what Hero Training Camp is all about. We're going to show you some small things you can do in your life so that you can be a hero every day. Watch the keys as I now let go of the paper clip."

This time, hold the paper clip out from your finger at a 90° angle with the keys dangling over your finger about one inch. When you release the paper clip give it a little push toward the floor. It will fall and then wrap around your finger, preventing the keys from hitting the ground.

For a more dramatic presentation you may even want to use one of the children's fingers in the demonstration.

Discussion points: The point is that just a small change can make all the difference. The same is true about heroes. David had one piece of information that others didn't have and it made all the difference in solving his problem.

★ ★ ★ ★ ★

Bible Story
A Hero Revealed

Use 1 Samuel 17 and the notes below to tell the Bible story.

You may have to change the wording to match the developmental level of the children you're working with.

When this story took place David was just a boy, probably a teenager. We know that because he wasn't considered old enough to join his brothers in the battle. The Philistines had been attacking the Israelites for some time. Now the Israelites faced their enemy in the valley of Elah. The Israelites lined up on one hill and the Philistines on the other and they were waiting. It was a standoff.

One of the soldiers from the Philistine camp came out and made fun of the Israelites, laughing at them. His name was Goliath and he was nine feet tall! (If the ceiling in your room is high enough, mark nine feet with a piece of tape and another place about five feet.) He was huge. Just his size frightened the Israelites. No one wanted to go out and fight him. No one!

David had been doing his job. Do you remember what his job was back at home? (Taking care of sheep.) Every day David was responsible and made sure that the sheep were okay, safe, and eating well. Last time we learned that when someone does what's right in the little things others begin to notice. Often it's the training in the little things that results in bigger opportunities. Now was that time, because Jesse, David's dad, had a job for David to do.

"I want you to take these loaves of bread and ten packages of cheese to the commander in the army. While you're there I want you to find out how your three older brothers are doing in the battle." Jesse was concerned for his sons who had gone off to fight the battle and he knew that he could trust David to go and get news and especially find out if his sons were okay.

So David headed off to the valley of Elah. He arrived on the scene just as the army was lining up to face the Philistines. David raced up to the front lines to ask his brothers how they were doing. Just then Goliath came out to insult the Israelites. David was shocked. Why wasn't anyone going out there to kill this enemy? Why was everyone so afraid?

Session 2 ★ Understanding the Mission

When David's brother Eliab saw David and heard him asking questions of the men, Eliab was suspicious of David. "I know you just came out here to see the battle. You should be at home taking care of those sheep."

But David continued to ask the other soldiers, "Why isn't someone going out there to kill Goliath?"

Someone told King Saul about David and Saul sent for him. David said to King Saul, "Why isn't anyone fighting Goliath? I'll go out and fight him." David was upset that Goliath was making fun of the Israelites. They were God's people. David knew that this was wrong and that someone needed to do something about it. If no one else would go out and fight this guy, David was willing to do it himself.

Saul said, "David, you're just a young guy. This man has been practicing his fighting since he was your age." Saul was a king but there was an important piece of information that Saul didn't have, but David did. Just like in our paper clip illustration, when you know the right things then you can do something great.

When David heard Saul talk about Goliath's training and ability, he remembered something very important. He remembered how God had already prepared him for this battle by giving him victory while he was taking care of the sheep. One time a lion came to attack his sheep, but God gave David victory over the lion. Another time a bear came to attack his sheep, but God gave David victory over the bear. God had prepared David to face this enemy because David had seen God work in his life several times before.

That's what happens in your life and my life too. God uses the struggles, challenges, and interruptions of our lives now to prepare us for something bigger. Do you know how to respond to those challenges now? Many kids aren't strong enough to face challenges. They just get angry. Kids who get angry miss out on the lessons for becoming a hero. We're going to help you today learn more about dealing with your own anger so that you can learn from the challenges that come your way.

Saul agreed to let David go and fight Goliath and

he had his men bring armor for David to wear. David put on the heavy armor and tried to walk around but he could hardly move. "I can't wear this stuff," he said. David knew that it wasn't what's on the outside that was most important but what's on the inside.

So David went out to the valley to face Goliath with just his regular clothes and his sling, oh and one more piece of information. David knew something that Goliath didn't know. David knew that God had prepared him for this battle, that God was on his side, and that even if he was small he could win because God would help him.

David went down to the bottom of the valley where the small stream was and he picked up five smooth stones. He then went out to face Goliath.

If you were Goliath, nine feet tall, with all kinds of armor on, what would you think if you saw young David coming out?

Goliath saw David and said, "What is this? Do you think I'm a dog and you are coming at me with sticks? Come over here and I'm going to turn you into animal food."

Just then David ran quickly toward Goliath. He took one of the stones out of his pouch, put it into his sling, and fired that stone right at Goliath's head. The stone hit him in the forehead and Goliath fell facedown on the ground. David ran over, took the heavy sword of Goliath, and cut off the giant's head.

David had rescued the Israelites. But that wasn't the first time he fought an enemy, was it? After all, God had helped David several times before so that David was ready to meet the challenge of the big giant.

It makes you wonder, doesn't it? What challenges are you facing right now that God can use to help you to be ready to face bigger challenges in life? Here are some answers that other children have given:

— I have a hard time with math. I just don't get it sometimes. I'm working hard to learn it and asking God to help me. Maybe if I can conquer the math, then God will use that victory in my life to help me face bigger struggles.

— My parents are getting a divorce. My heart hurts because of it. Sometimes I'm angry but mostly I'm disappointed and sad. I wonder if God will be able to use me. I'm trusting God to help me get through this experience so that I can be strong on the inside.

I don't know what your current struggles are, but I want you to know that God wants to do great things in your life. Heroes don't just wake up one morning and find themselves strong. They grow over time by meeting challenges of life over and over again. You too can stand up to those challenges in your own life.

Two things happened to David. First he became uncomfortable with what he saw happening with Goliath. Then he trusted God to help him. God uses your conscience to help you see things that need to be done. Then the next step is to trust him to work in and through you to accomplish something big.

Take away: I face challenges every day and, if I learn from them, I'll be able to handle bigger challenges later on in life.

Bible Verse
James 1:2-3
Consider it pure joy, my brothers, whenever you face trials of many kinds, because you know that the testing of your faith develops perseverance.

★ ★ ★ ★ ★

Game
Potato Race

Supplies needed: Spoons, potatoes, bowls, and a camera

Instructions: Children must scoop a potato from a bowl on one table and carry it to the other table and place it in the bowl. Children can form teams and half of their team starts at one table and half at the other table providing a relay race feel.

With a smaller group use a stopwatch and race the clock. With a larger number of children you might have two or three groups racing at the same time; the excitement often causes children to move faster than they are able, illustrating an important point: When things get intense you have to slow down instead of going faster.

In order for this activity to communicate its point, strict guidelines must be followed.

- The children must keep one hand behind their backs and their other hand at least two inches from the potato.

- If the potato misses the bowl, falls on the ground, or is touched by either hand, then the child must stop and move backwards one step, and regroup before continuing.

It's important to enforce these rules to illustrate the point of this activity.

For older children you may use a teaspoon and with younger children you may want to use serving spoons.

Take pictures to display later.

Discussion points: The potato race uses emotion to motivate a person to push ahead even when it's not the best solution. Anger in everyday situations has the same effect and the solution to anger tendencies is always to slow down or stop and settle down before continuing. Unfortunately, the anger often makes a child want to push forward instead of pulling back. That's when people get hurt or relationships get strained.

After the potato races have the children gather together and explain the lesson learned from the game. What is the secret of getting the potato from one side to the other without dropping it? What happens if you go too fast? What makes you want to go faster?

Here's the hero lesson we learn from this activity. In the potato race, the intensity makes you want to push forward faster than you really are able to. In life, there is an emotion that many children face that hinders their abilities. It's anger. But, if you can learn to deal with your anger and not let it push you forward, then you can be a more successful hero.

Anger is an emotion that provides extra energy, but that energy can lead to trouble by saying something unkind or hurting someone with words or actions. One of the keys to managing anger is to slow down or even stop and step back for a moment.

The problem is that you don't feel like stepping back. You feel like pushing forward. That's where practice comes in. When you start to feel angry, stop, take a deep breath, and pause for a moment. Keeping yourself under control is one of the signs of a hero. If you practice the skill of slowing down your anger, you'll be doing what the Bible says in James 1:19, "Be quick to listen, slow to speak, and slow to become angry." That's an important skill for any hero.

Do the potato race again to allow children to practice keeping themselves under control. Repeating the race allows children to learn from success, not just learn from failure.

Conscience Insight

Angry people are unhappy people because the conscience continues to remind them that they've lost control and acted inappropriately. Furthermore, anger often confuses the problem solving process. People who use anger to solve problems often hurt others and damage relation-ships.

It's important to learn to manage anger well to become a hero. Heroes can see something that's wrong. That's a good quality. However, when people blame or mistreat others because they are angry, more offenses take place. A hero knows how to keep anger under control and approach problems with more effective solutions.

Role Play
David Kills Goliath

Use the ideas below to help children act out what the story of David and Goliath might have been like. Depending on the children, you may want to narrate more or less of the story, thus allowing the kids with a greater comfort level with drama to carry the story on their own, while others may need more coaching.

As you introduce each character take pictures to display later.

Choose three children to play David's brothers. They were sent to the battlefield to help Israel fight against the Philistines. (Have the brothers look tough like soldiers.)

Choose an adult leader to play Goliath. This will avoid having a child play the negative role and will give the leader an opportunity to act out a dramatic death. Goliath came out each day and taunted the Israelites, challenging them to come out and fight him. (Goliath, show your stuff.)

Choose a child to play David. David was sent on an errand to bring some food to his brothers and to check on the battle. But when he got there Goliath came out to make fun of the Israelites. (David, look responsible.)

Choose another child to play King Saul. (Look kingly.) David went and talked to Saul to get permission to fight the giant. David told Saul about his victory over the lion and the bear. "God will give me victory over this giant."

Saul was willing but wanted to prepare David by having him wear armor. Of course, the armor was too heavy for David and he decided to fight without it.

David went down to the little river and chose five smooth stones. He put one in his sling and rushed toward Goliath. He let one stone fly and it hit Goliath right in the forehead. The giant fell down dead. David quickly went over and cut off his head.

Discussion points: Have children sit down and ask them the following questions:

How do you think David felt when he saw Goliath making fun of the Israelites?

How do you think he felt with all that armor on?

What was it that made David confident that he could go out and challenge the giant?

What are things you do in your home that are important now, but prepare you for bigger things later on? For example, cleaning up your toys helps you learn to be neat and work hard.

With older children you might engage them in discussion about bullies.

What are some ways that kids are bullies today?

What are some ways to respond to kids who bully? Answers might include ignoring, reporting it to an authority, or confronting the bully. The important thing to realize is that bullies have problems on the inside and they are pretending to be strong outwardly in order to hide their internal weakness.

Repeat the theme from this session:
Difficulties in life make heroes stronger to prepare them for handling bigger challenges that may come their way.

★ ★ ★ ★ ★

Game
The Anger Bomb Game

Supplies needed: Photocopy for each child the two game pages from the end of this lesson (pages 54 and 55). Also provide paper lunch bags in which to take the game home.

Instructions: Using the pages at the end of this lesson, have each child finish cutting the two bombs, fuses, and game cards. For younger children you may want to do some cutting ahead of time, especially the slit at the top of the bomb where the fuse goes in. Remind children to cut the whole fuse out as one strip and not to cut it into pieces. Show them a finished example of what it looks like before they cut out the game. Place the game cards in the paper lunch bag.

To play the game: Children should each have a partner. Using just one of their game sets, the two children mix the game cards in the bag. Each child gets one of the bombs and inserts a fuse into the top, pushing it down to the midpoint where it says START HERE.

Explain to the children that the longer the fuse is, the more time it has before the bomb explodes. The objective of the game is to actually pull the fuse farther and farther out until it is removed. That person is the winner because they have avoided the explosion.

The first child takes a turn by reaching into the bag and taking one card out and reading it out loud. If it has a small bomb on it then it's something that children say to themselves that increase, their anger. The child must push the fuse one step into their bomb. The fuse is getting shorter, illustrating that an explosion is getting closer. If the child chooses a SUPER SOLUTION card, the fuse is pulled out one step illustrating that the explosion is further away.

Children alternate taking turns, picking cards until one of the children has either "exploded" or has successfully removed the fuse. If all the cards are used up before the end of the game, take the cards, mix them up again, and put them back into the bag to continue play.

49

Session 2 ★ Understanding the Mission

If a child's fuse goes all the way in, then his bomb "explodes" and he has to say these words, "Oops I lost it. I need to take a Break."

If a child successfully removes the fuse then he wins and says, "Yes, I CAN handle my anger."

For preschoolers: Play the game as one large group. Explain how the game is played and have one child at a time come up and pick a card. Read the card to the group and have that same child move the fuse in or out. When the game ends have the group together make the final statement. Talk about anger and use some of the discussion points below.

Discussion points: One of the ways to manage anger is to know what to say to yourself when you're starting to get angry. Many kids say things like, "It's not fair," "I'm going to get back at you," which actually make them feel more angry. In fact, when kids say the word "should" to themselves about situations and other people then anger is often the result.

Heroes know how to keep their anger under control. In order to do that, they often say things to calm themselves down. Practice saying the words from the SUPER SOLUTION cards to yourself to prevent your anger from exploding.

Managing anger takes practice and requires self-control. You might want to share the verse from Proverbs 25:28, "Like a city whose walls are broken down is a man who lacks self-control." The point of this verse is that even a mighty city loses its strength when its walls fall down. A person who can't manage anger is like a city with no walls. Walls help a city to be strong and protected. The person who can't control anger is weak.

Self-control is part of the fruit of the Spirit. Children can pray and ask God to help them when they are tempted to act out in anger.

When you're done with this activity, have children put all the pieces in their bags and put their names on them. Place the bags along the wall to take home later.

You might want to make this activity ongoing in your home by adding some signal words to family interaction. Identify "Bomb Busters" as words that incite anger and flare tempers. On the other hand, "Super Solutions" are words that describe ideas children have that reduce anger and frustration. Family members may use these words to describe their own control or they may be used to describe the responses of others. You might even take it a step further by making sounds such as a fuse or an explosion to lighten a situation that is intensifying. At the same time when a child provides a solution you could throw a spontaneous hero parade with whooping and cheering.

Establishing cues or signals is a creative way to reduce the typical parental prompters and encourage children to see anger and solutions to anger for themselves.

★ ★ ★ ★ ★

Hero Field Guide

Supplies needed: The Hero Field Guides made in the previous lesson. Also photocopy the verse for today on page 57, plus glue, and crayons or markers. For preschoolers you may want to use the Hero Color Sheet on page 56 instead.

Talk about the Bible verse as you add it to the second page of the guide. You might use some of these ideas to help guide the conversation.

Discussion points: Problems happen to everyone. The Bible tells us how to view problems that come into our lives. How do you feel when Mom or Dad tells you to stop playing a video game or stop a movie in the middle and go clean something up? Interruptions can be frustrating, can't they? For a hero, interruptions are the mission. Heroes overcome their frustration and respond well to the challenge.

How would you feel if you got an assignment from school that was especially tough, harder than you're used to? Some would become discouraged and feel hopeless. Heroes take on the challenge, get help, and move forward, working hard to get the job done.

This Bible verse reminds us of the way that heroes approach problems and interruptions in their lives.

Glue the verse on the page. Before you leave this activity, read the whole page to the kids. Then collect the Field Guides and keep them for the next lesson.

✶ ✶ ✶ ✶ ✶

Craft
A Sling Shot

Supplies needed:
Knee-high stockings (one stocking for each child), sand, plastic sandwich bags, rubber bands (2 per child), permanent felt pen, and scissors

Instructions: Put 1 tablespoon of sand in a plastic sandwich bag and seal it shut with a rubber band, leaving the sand loose instead of tight for more flexibility. Cut off the rest of the plastic or wrap it around the 'sand ball' for added security. Depending on the age of the child, children may need help with this portion. In fact, you may want to prepare the plastic wrapped sand in advance to cut down on the time spent in this activity.

Put a 'sand ball' in the toe of a knee-high stocking. Twist the stocking three times about a 1/2″ above

the sand, then push the whole toe through the stocking. Twist three times about 1/2″ above the base again and push it through the stocking. Repeat for a total of three times and then use a rubber band to secure it. By leaving about 1/2″ above the sand you allow more flexibility in the sand, making it softer and more flexible when it reaches its mark. If the sand is packed too tightly it becomes harder and might hurt someone on impact. At the top of the sling, spread out the nylon and, with a piece of paper underneath, write the child's name using a permanent felt pen. The sling is now ready to use.

How to use the sling: An early Israelite sling that may have been used by David wasn't like our slingshot today. Instead, it was held in one hand, had two pieces of leather, and a stone was placed in a fold at the end. After spinning it around several times to gain speed, one of the ends was released freeing the stone to move forward. The sling created in this lesson is a little different but it uses the same principle of swinging it around before releasing it toward your target.

Practice using the slings. Take pictures to display later. Create a few targets around the room. One might be trying to get the sling to land in a trash can. Another might be a target on the wall. Another might be a box of tissues on the end of a table. Allow the children to practice using their slings to hit the target.

With slings flying around the room this activity can get out of hand. Be sure to set up some ground rules early. You might have one group practice first while the other group keeps their slings on the table without touching them. Or you may establish a guideline that allows children to try their slings but when you stay STOP then everyone sits down with their sling in front of them, not touching it.

Discussion points: It's not easy to use a sling, is it? It takes a lot of practice. In fact David must have spent hours practicing. Heroes have to practice many things in order to move to the next level. Do any of you do martial arts like karate? (If so, ask what belt the child has earned.) The reality is that if you want to be good at what you do then you have to practice and, over time, you get better at it.

When you're done with this activity, have children put their slings along the wall with their Anger Bomb Game to take home.

Hero Skill Building Activity
Going Toe-to-Toe

Supplies needed: A camera

Instructions: Each child pairs up with another child about their same size. Children face each other, putting the outside of their right foot alongside the outside of their partner's right foot. Then they raise their right hand and grasp the right hand of their partner. When the leader says go, the two "wrestle" by pushing and pulling with the one hand until one of the players moves the right foot or falls to the ground. The left foot can move to provide some stability.

Take pictures to display later.

Some children will appreciate this kind of activity more than others, hopefully pairing up with partners who share their same level of interest. After allowing everyone the opportunity to try the activity, you may find it helpful to have the children sit down and have challenges between some of the winners. Competition has its advantages and disadvantages. So allowing children who don't want to compete to sit and watch can alleviate

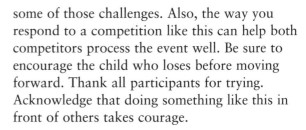

some of those challenges. Also, the way you respond to a competition like this can help both competitors process the event well. Be sure to encourage the child who loses before moving forward. Thank all participants for trying. Acknowledge that doing something like this in front of others takes courage.

Discussion points: What enables you to win? (Pushing the person off balance and maintaining your own balance.) Balance is the key ingredient. The same thing is true emotionally. Some people are easily thrown off balance. One of the keys to being a hero is to keep yourself under control and not letting someone else control your emotions. Anger is a problem and can rob you of balance. Others then control you. For example, if you have a brother who likes to make you angry then, when he is successful at getting you upset, he has control over you. Your goal as a hero is to maintain your inner control even when others are trying to get you upset. God helps you do that using the Holy Spirit to remind you to do the right thing.

Snack
David's Five Stones

Supplies needed: Honey Nut Cheerios, bananas, a knife, and a ziplock bag for each child

Instructions: Slice the bananas into round pieces. Place a 1/2 cup of Honey Nut Cheerios in each ziplock bag. Squeeze the air out and allow the children to smash the cheerios into crumbs with their hands. This step actually takes a bit of work and younger children might benefit from using a utensil such as a wooden block or blunt object. Next, distribute five banana slices (rounds) to each child. The child can put the banana slices into the plastic bag, shake it up, and then eat them. Have extra bananas available for children who would like more.

Discussion points: David took five stones with him to fight Goliath. Let's go back and look at the story of David and Goliath for a moment. What is the lesson we're learning from the story? David learned how to respond to challenges of the lion and the bear before he was able to face the giant. In the same way the current challenges we face can prepare us for greater challenges later. Our job is to respond well. What are some challenges kids face today? Interruptions, irritations, parents say no, difficult chores, disappointments, etc. How do those challenges help kids for the future? What is a better response than anger to the challenges of life?

★ ★ ★ ★ ★

HERO Exercise

As you practice at home, look for ways to respond well to problems, interruptions, and challenges. See if you can reduce anger by keeping yourself under control. You might pull back instead of push forward or use some statements to calm yourself down. Report back at the next lesson and we'll see how you did.

★ ★ ★ ★ ★

Conclusion

Most people look at the story of David and Goliath all by itself. They don't look at what happened before and after that story and they miss a very important lesson. David faced smaller challenges in his life before he met Goliath. God does the same thing with us.

One of the big problems that gets in the way is an angry response to the challenges people face. I'd like a volunteer to come up to help me with a demonstration.

Choose one child and give these instructions. "Put your feet together and see if you can stand strong when I try to push you over. Are you ready?" Give a small push and watch the child easily lose

balance. Then say, "Now, I want you to put your feet about shoulder width apart, bend your knees, and get ready like a football player. See if I can push you over. Are you ready?" Give a push but not strong enough to push the child over.

That's how you want to respond to people on the inside. You have to be ready so that people aren't knocking you over all the time. The person who gets angry a lot doesn't have the internal balance necessary to manage life.

Take some time and develop this part of being a hero. It will help you greatly to meet the challenges of your life both now and for the future.

SEEING IT THROUGH THE EYES OF A CHILD

"It's like the levels on my video game. I can get angry at having to do a level over and over again. Or I can see it as a way to become better. It's the same as life. I can see the small stuff as a way to become better."

— Brian, age 10

★ ★ ★ ★ ★

Prayer

Dear Lord, thank you for giving us your Holy Spirit to guide us and remind us to do what's right. We know that you can help us have self-control on the inside even when we face challenges on the outside. I want to pray for each of these children that you would give them the ability to see challenges like you see them. Help them to respond well to the interruptions and problems of their lives. Amen.

Session 2 ★ Understanding the Mission

The Anger Bomb Game

Fuses

Oops I lost it. I need to take a Break	Oops I lost it. I need to take a Break
start here	start here
Yes. I CAN handle my anger	Yes. I CAN handle my anger

I can't stand it when my dad tells me I did something wrong.

I get mad when I can't find my shoe.

It makes me mad when my friend won't play with me.

I hate it when Mom says "No."

Mom shouldn't tell me I can't watch TV.

Being teased makes me mad.

I don't like being interrupted.

I'm annoyed when my brother keeps bothering me.

SUPER SOLUTION I will hang in there and keep going without getting upset.

SUPER SOLUTION I can ignore this and not let it get to me.

SUPER SOLUTION I just need to settle down.

SUPER SOLUTION I can wait. It's no big deal.

SUPER SOLUTION This isn't worth getting angry about.

SUPER SOLUTION I don't have to get all worked up about this.

SUPER SOLUTION Take three deep breaths slowly.

SUPER SOLUTION This is disappointing but I can deal with it.

PROBLEMS
AND CHALLENGES
ARE MY MISSION

Consider it pure
joy, my brothers,
whenever
you face trials of
many kinds,
because you know
that the testing
of your faith
develops
perseverance.

James 1:2-3

Consider it pure
joy, my brothers,
whenever
you face trials of
many kinds,
because you know
that the testing
of your faith
develops
perseverance.

James 1:2-3

Consider it pure
joy, my brothers,
whenever
you face trials of
many kinds,
because you know
that the testing
of your faith
develops
perseverance.

James 1:2-3

Consider it pure
joy, my brothers,
whenever
you face trials of
many kinds,
because you know
that the testing
of your faith
develops
perseverance.

James 1:2-3

NATIONAL CENTER
for BIBLICAL
Parenting

76 Hopatcong Drive, Lawrenceville, NJ 08648-4136
(800) 771-8334 or (609) 771-8002
Email: parent@biblicalparenting.org
Web: biblicalparenting.org

God Prepares Heroes to Fight the Giants

Dear Parent,

Each lesson in **Hero Training Camp** teaches one story from the life of David. In this lesson children learned about David and Goliath. In particular we saw that current challenges often prepare us for bigger challenges in the future. David killed a lion and a bear before God used him to face a giant. Children learned that challenges, problems, and interruptions in their lives provide opportunities to practice responding well.

In this session we spent extra time talking about a poor response to challenges in order to help children see that they have a choice. We talked about anger and some practical ways to work on controlling it.

As you see anger in your children one of the key ways to help them gain control is to keep calm yourself. Although anger in children often raises the anger level in parents, your control in those situations keeps the problem the child's problem.

Furthermore, when children get angry they want to push forward, usually resulting in hurt to others. One of the best ways to help children develop self-control is to require that they pull back instead of push forward. This may be tough at first, especially when a child reacts with a tantrum, but when you refuse to join the anger episode and require that the child settle down before returning to the activities, you're teaching a valuable lesson and important skill.

Anger in children can be quite difficult. Your response to anger episodes though can go a long way to help children develop the internal control they need. Have discussions about anger and talk about practical ways to decrease it. Over time you'll see children decrease the frequency and intensity of anger episodes.

The **Bible verse** is James 1:2-3, "Consider it pure joy, my brothers, whenever you face trials of many kinds, because you know that the testing of your faith develops perseverance." (Preschool children worked on verse 2 only.)

The **Power Words** are, "Problems, interruptions, and challenges are my mission." Children were given a **Hero Exercise** for this lesson to look for ways to respond well to interruptions, problems, and challenges. In particular they were encouraged to work on anger control by pulling back instead of pushing forward when they feel angry.

Heroes have the ability to handle challenges with internal control. Both the conscience and the Holy Spirit provide resources to help children develop self-control. Look for ways to coach your child in this area this week.

Blessings,

Scott Turansky

Joanne Miller

How a **HERO** Knows What's Right

Preparing Your Heart to Teach Session 3

One of the things that helps people do what's right and fight temptation is convictions. These beliefs become the inner rules upon which decisions and choices are based. Unfortunately, many children don't make choices based on conviction but use emotion instead. In this lesson children will learn what convictions are and how they can rely on them in life.

All children have convictions but many of those things children believe are wrong. For example, one child might believe that he is entitled to revenge when offended. That conviction can lead to significant conflict. Part of the job of parents and teachers is to help children develop convictions that come from God's Word. That's a life-long process but it starts now in the everyday activities of life.

One of the reasons we are all attracted to heroes is because they take a stand for what's right. Daniel, for example, "purposed in his heart that he would not defile himself" with the king's food (Daniel 1:8). Heroes have beliefs on the inside that help them make right choices. They have convictions that help them overcome evil, address their own personal temptations, and do the right thing.

One of the goals of this lesson is to help children see that they too can be heroes and convictions are a necessary ingredient. Convictions provide direction for the conscience and help with the many choices one faces each day.

Supplies Needed for This Lesson

Square Puzzle
Supplies needed: Photocopy the puzzle on pages 71 and 72, front and back on a piece of card stock, and provide one puzzle for every two children. Cut the puzzle into pieces.

Dancing Raisins
Supplies needed: Clear soda like club soda or Sprite, a drinking glass, and about 10 raisins

Bible Story
Supplies needed: Belief cards from pages 74-76.

Emotions vs. Convictions
Supplies needed (optional): You may want to provide props for the children as they try to act out these scenarios, a stuffed animal or doll, a handheld video game, and a board game.

Hero Field Guide
Supplies needed: The Hero Field Guides from the previous lesson and page 83 photocopied and cut for each child, glue, and crayons or markers

Convictions Game
Supplies needed: Photocopy onto card stock pages 77 and 78 for each child. You'll also need scissors and small plastic bags to hold the game pieces for the children to take home.

Code Breaker Wheel
Supplies needed: Photocopy the Code Breaker page and the Code Breaker Wheel page on pages 79 and 80, one set for each child. You'll also need a brad for each child and scissors. (If working with preschoolers, use the maze on page 81 instead.)

Trail Mix Buffet
Supplies needed: Raisins, mini pretzels, O-shaped cereal, banana chips, Chex cereal, and any other ingredient you would like to add

or substitute for one on this list. You'll also need one serving bowl for each ingredient, serving spoons for each ingredient, and a small plastic bag for each child.

Conclusion
Supplies needed: Compass

Other suggested items:
- Photocopy the Parent Letter for each student.
- Be prepared to play the Hero Song if you have the Hero Training Camp Music CD.
- Have a camera ready to take pictures.

Theme

Heroes rely on inner beliefs called convictions that help them make right choices.

Power Words

I will develop convictions based on God's Word.

Theological Truth

Convictions based on God's Word provide my conscience with direction, freedom, and power.

Welcome Activity
Square Puzzle

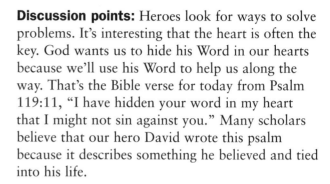

Supplies needed:
Photocopy the puzzle on pages 71 and 72, front and back on a piece of card stock, and provide one puzzle for every two children. Cut the puzzle into pieces.

Instructions: As children come in, greet them and then encourage them to work in pairs to complete the puzzle using the side without the heart. The goal is to assemble the pieces to form a square. If they are having trouble they can turn all the pieces over and use the heart shape to provide some clues.

Discussion points: Heroes look for ways to solve problems. It's interesting that the heart is often the key. God wants us to hide his Word in our hearts because we'll use his Word to help us along the way. That's the Bible verse for today from Psalm 119:11, "I have hidden your word in my heart that I might not sin against you." Many scholars believe that our hero David wrote this psalm because it describes something he believed and tied into his life.

Today we are going to explore some things that you believe in your heart. Some of those things are good and some are not. Heroes have the ability to solve puzzles in life, even though they may have trouble solving them in a game. The key to solving the puzzles in life has to do with what they believe in their hearts. That's why this lesson is so important.

For preschoolers: Also photocopy the Puzzle Game Board on page 73 but don't cut it out. Have the young children turn all of the puzzle pieces so that the lines for the heart are face up. As children place the pieces of the puzzle onto the template, the heart shape is revealed.

Together Time

I will LISTEN with my 👁 👁, Keep my mouth UNDER CONTROL, Do what the teacher SAYS, knowing that becoming a HERO for God is MY GOAL.

Gather together and remind children of the Hero Training Creed. Take a few moments to help children calm down and prepare their hearts with a prayer, asking God to settle the hearts and provide opportunity to focus on today's training. Review the Hero Exercise that the children were assigned in the previous session. In our last session we talked about handling interruptions well without getting angry. Can you tell us a time when you were able to do that?

Hero Training Creed:
> I will listen with my eyes, keep my mouth under control, do what the teacher says, knowing that becoming a hero for God is my goal.

★ ★ ★ ★ ★

Introduction
Dancing Raisins

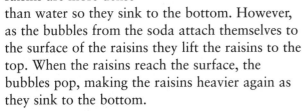

Supplies needed: Clear soda like club soda or Sprite, a drinking glass, and about 10 raisins

Instructions: Fill the glass with the soda. Add the raisins. They will fall to the bottom, and then watch what happens.

Why it works: The raisins are more dense than water so they sink to the bottom. However, as the bubbles from the soda attach themselves to the surface of the raisins they lift the raisins to the top. When the raisins reach the surface, the bubbles pop, making the raisins heavier again as they sink to the bottom.

Discussion points: Heroes are different than other people. Heroes tend to rise up to the surface in life. What we mean by that is that they stand out from others. They are different. When something needs to be done, the hero steps out and does it. That's why we say he rises to the top. In the same way that the raisins have bubbles that float them to the surface, kids with convictions stand out.

The bubbles on the raisins are like convictions. Convictions are internal beliefs that your conscience relies on to make decisions. They are rules in our hearts that tell us what we should do. Today in our story we're going to learn more about convictions and how they helped David in difficult situations.

For preschoolers: Young children will enjoy this activity. Talk about convictions in terms of "beliefs in your heart that make you do the right thing." You might say, "Let's imagine that these raisins are like people wanting to get to the top. They need to do the right thing. Do you see the

little bubbles that attach themselves to the raisins? That's like doing the right thing and see what happens? The raisin comes to the top. When you do the right thing you can move forward as well."

★ ★ ★ ★ ★

Bible Story
It Does Make a Difference
What You Believe

Supplies needed: Belief cards from pages 74-76.

This Bible story is taken from 1 Samuel 18-20. Use the Bible and the following thoughts to teach the story and the lesson to the children. You may have to change the wording or explanations to match the developmental level of the children you're working with.

In our story today we're going to talk about beliefs that David had. Those beliefs will help him make wise choices and even help him do the right thing when life gets tough. See if you can help me identify some of the beliefs. (Use the cards at the end of this lesson to help you identify beliefs during this story.)

David became quite popular after he killed Goliath. King Saul was impressed with this young man and even offered him a job. Saul hired David to play his harp-like guitar in the palace so that whenever Saul felt bad, the music would cheer him up.

When David was in the palace he met Saul's son, Jonathan. They had a lot in common and soon became good friends. They would play together, talk all the time, and share ideas, dreams, and plans with each other. They loved each other a lot. David knew in his heart that he and Jonathan were friends. (Tape belief card #1 up on the wall.)

David shared with Jonathan about the time that the prophet Samuel came to his house and told him that he would be king someday. Jonathan was so happy for David even though it meant that David would be king instead of Jonathan who was the king's son. (Tape belief card #2 up on the wall.)

Over time their friendship grew and grew. David and Jonathan didn't know what was going to happen but they did know that they were life-long friends. That belief that they were committed to each other would help them in a way they didn't realize.

You see, David's popularity began to grow throughout the whole country. In fact, some of the young ladies made up a song. Although we don't know the tune, the words compared David's success in battle with the king's. The words said, "Saul has killed thousands, but David has killed ten thousands." Saul heard those words and began to feel jealous of David. In fact, Saul became angry because the people liked David so much. Saul decided to kill David.

The very next day while David was playing his music in Saul's bedroom, Saul started thinking about how angry and jealous he was and he took his spear that was next to his bed and he threw it at David to try to kill him. David jumped out of the way. Saul continued to look for ways to hurt David. I'm sure that David was very upset by all of this. But instead of getting angry he was able to trust God. What belief do you think helped him make that decision? (Reveal belief card #3 and tape it up on the wall.)

Because Saul tried to kill him, David ran away. He went to Jonathan and told him what had happened. Jonathan couldn't believe it. "Surely my father is not trying to kill you."

David said, "Here's how you can help me. Tomorrow is a special dinner when I'm supposed

to eat with the king. Instead of going to the party I'll hide out here in the field. See if my absence makes the king angry. If it does, we'll know that he is trying to kill me."

Jonathan agreed. Then they developed a secret plan. Jonathan said, "Tomorrow afternoon I'll come out here to the field and pretend to do some shooting practice with my bow and arrow. You hide by that big rock. I'll shoot three arrows and then send a boy after them. If I yell to the boy, 'The arrows are closer, come back this way,' then that means everything is okay and you can come back safely. However, if I say to the boy, the arrows are farther away go farther, then that means that you should run away because you were right. My father is trying to kill you."

So, the next day David waited by the big rock. It wasn't long before he heard Jonathan coming out to practice shooting arrows. He was waiting to hear what Jonathan would say. Arrows flew into the air. The boy went to get them. David listened. He heard Jonathan yell to the boy, "The arrow is farther on. Go quickly. Don't stop." David's heart dropped. Oh no. What he had imagined was true. The boy found the arrow. Jonathan gave him the arrows and the bow and told the boy to go back to the palace.

Before David could leave, Jonathan went out to meet him. They were crying because they knew that David had to run for his life. Jonathan told David how the king had been so angry that David wasn't at the party the night before. Surely Saul would have tried to kill him at the party. They were both very sad. David had to leave.

David hadn't done anything wrong but he was being mistreated by King Saul. That same problem of being mistreated happens to children sometimes. Maybe it's even happened to you.

- Robert's coach only let him play for one inning then he took him out of the baseball game. All the other kids got to play at least three innings and some played the whole game. Robert was disappointed.

- Adam's teacher told the whole class that she was disappointed that Adam didn't turn in his paper on time. There were other kids who didn't turn in their papers but the teacher singled him out. Adam was embarrassed.

These situations seem to be unfair. But how the kids respond to those situations is so important. One response to being hurt is that kids can get very angry. In fact, they can get so angry inside that their anger starts to affect them and turn them into angry people. That's dangerous.

David, in our story, didn't let that happen to him. In fact, he was able to continue to do what's right and trust the Lord even when he was mistreated like he was. He was able to do that because he believed some things in his heart. Those things are called convictions. David knew that God wanted him to be king. David also knew in his heart that Jonathan was a real friend to him. He also knew that God is in control. (Review the three beliefs we've identified.)

Convictions are very important to heroes. In fact, heroes do what's right because of beliefs that they hold. Let's talk about some beliefs that you might have.

• Rhonda is clearing her lunch tray at school and when she gets to the trash, just throws it all, including the can from her soda, right into the trash. Her friend Mary stops her and says, "Wait, that can goes over here in the recycling." What conviction does Mary have that prompts her to take the can out of the trash and put it into the recycling? (Add the belief card in a new column on the wall.)

• Randy's friends are in a store and they are looking for a way to take some gum without paying for it. Randy walks away and goes home. What conviction do you think Randy holds? (Add the belief card to the wall that says "Stealing is wrong.")

Who can think of another belief example that a child might have? (Write the answer on the last belief card.) This question will likely be difficult for children so if you get no response, be ready with your own idea such as, "Helping out around the house is everyone's job," or, "I need to help out when I see someone hurt."

Heroes have convictions. That means that they believe things and they take a stand for what they believe. Sometimes it's a stand for doing something that's honest. Other times it's a conviction to make a wrong right, or care for someone else.

In our lesson today we will explore some of the convictions you might have or want to develop. We'll also talk about how convictions help us deal with the issue of being mistreated when someone is unkind or mean.

Take away: Convictions based on God's Word provide my conscience with direction, freedom, and power.

For preschoolers: The whole idea of convictions will be tough for young children to understand. It may be helpful to talk about what's right and what's wrong. This concrete approach to beliefs often connects with young children. For example, in the recycling illustration, most preschoolers can understand that the cans go in a different place, the right place, even though they may not understand a conviction behind that idea.

Bible Verse
Psalm 119:11
I have hidden your word in my heart that I might not sin against you.

★ ★ ★ ★ ★

Role Play
Emotions vs. Convictions

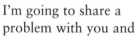

Supplies needed (optional): You may want to provide props for the children as they try to act out these scenarios, a stuffed animal or doll, a handheld video game, and a board game.

I'm going to share a problem with you and you will act out an emotional response, which is often unhelpful and just creates a bigger problem. And then we'll act out a response that's based on what's right, a conviction.

Take pictures of children acting out the various role plays to show later.

For preschoolers: Story #1 is good for preschoolers, although you may want to use the words "right" and "wrong" instead of convictions to help illustrate the truth.

Story #1: The Three Sisters
Three characters needed: three siblings (You can change this to three boys or a mix of boys and girls if that's helpful.)

Three sisters were playing together and taking turns with the toy. Everything seemed to be going fine until it was Abigail's turn. The other girls changed the rules though so that Abigail didn't get a turn. She was hurt.

We need three girls to be the sisters. One will be Abigail. Pretend this is a toy and you're agreeing to take turns and then when it comes to Abigail's turn, change the rules. Abigail is sad. Now girls, you have a problem since your sister is sad. The first way I want you to act this out is by being selfish and wanting the toy for yourselves. You don't feel like sharing with Abigail. Go ahead, act that out.

Okay, this time instead of acting on emotions, we're going to act based on convictions. What are some convictions that the sisters could have that would result in a better response? Maybe the conviction is that we want others to feel good too. Or that sharing is the right thing. This time do the whole role play again including changing the rules so that Abigail doesn't get a turn but when she is sad then you can end up talking to each other about convictions and choose to do what's right.

Story #2: The Video Game
Two characters needed: a mom and a son

Mom is tired. She is trying to make dinner and the laundry didn't get done today. Go ahead Mom, be busy making dinner in a tired way. Billy wants to play with his video game. After all, he finally got his homework done. Now he's tired and really wants some video time. Here you go Billy, play away. If he acts on emotion, then the feelings are "being tired" and "wanting to be entertained." Mom turns to Billy and asks him to fold the laundry. First, let's hear Billy respond poorly based simply on his emotions. Mom and Billy can persist in their dialogue for a bit and let's see what happens.

Next, let's ask what conviction might Billy have that would result in a different response? A conviction might be, "I love Mom and she's tired and so I'll care for her by doing what she asks." Or the conviction might be, "Here's a family job that needs to get done and it looks like it's my turn to do this one. I'll work and then I'll play." OK, let's rewind the story and play it again. Watch how Billy responds differently with his words and his actions and then watch how Mom responds.

Story #3:
The Game is Over
Three characters needed:

three friends (You can change the gender and the names if that's helpful.)

James is playing a board game with his two friends. James lost the game and so one of the friends throws down his pieces and said, "Since you lost, you have to clean it up." James now feels hurt that his friend makes him clean up the game. He's angry and his friend even laughs about it. James continues to clean up the game while the friends talk about it. First, let's let the friends respond based on emotion. They are delighted that they didn't lose the game and didn't have to clean up. They also feel justified in having James do the clean-up, after all, he lost. Let's see this role play from the beginning.

Now, let's rewind the role play and see the boys act in a better way based on convictions. What conviction might they have that would end up with a different response? Maybe the boys would believe that because James is sad, they should apologize to him. Or maybe they would believe that cleaning up the game is really everyone's job. "We all help to clean up." Now let's replay the story having a right response based on conviction.

Discussion points: Heroes need to be careful not to react simply on emotion, but need to rely on convictions instead. What are some of the emotions that can get in the way of doing the right thing? Anger, fear, feeling tired, jealousy. That's why it's so important to have convictions in our hearts that drive us forward. Let's imagine that you're my friend and you're giving me advice to do the right thing. I'll make an emotion statement and you tell me why I should do the right thing, that is the conviction statement.

- I'm too tired to finish my homework.
- I'm angry with my sister. I'm going to get her back.
- I know I did the wrong thing but I don't want to admit it because I'm afraid of the punishment.
- I want to have some candy now so I'm just going to take it out of Mom's purse.

Feelings can get us into trouble sometimes. That's why convictions are so important. A hero spends a lot of time thinking about convictions and beliefs in order to make wise choices.

Conscience Insight

Rules are based on convictions. Rules are external prompters but convictions are internal prompters. The goal is to help children develop internal rules or convictions that will guide their behavior. One of the ways to do this is to have discussions about rules, asking children and adults to identify the convictions behind them. For example, one rule is that everyone comes to dinner whether they are hungry or not. Why? Because we have a conviction that meal times are social times, not just eating times. Analyze rules with children to help identify the convictions behind the rules.

★ ★ ★ ★ ★

Hero Skill Building Activity
The Human Chair

In this activity we want to imagine that you and two of your friends are up in the mountains in a cabin and while you're there, one of you steps in a hole and breaks his leg. Your job is to get down off the mountain. What I'm telling you is one of the things that rescue workers need to know, so as a hero in training, you better pay attention. Here's how you can move that person to safety.

Have a camera ready to take pictures of the children working together.

Instructions: Select two children to create a chair with their arms that the "hurt" child can sit on. Have these two children face each other, standing an arm's length apart. Have both children stretch out their right arms straight in front. Then have them hold out their left arms but bent at the elbow. Each child should lock his left hand onto his right elbow. Then have each child hold the other child's left elbow with his right hand, thus forming a square between them with their four forearms. This becomes the seat of the rescue chair. Have the two children bend down a bit so that the hurt child can sit on the seat they have created. Then the "hurt" child sits on the seat and puts his arms around the necks of the two who are carrying.

To practice this emergency procedure, we're going to have some races. Get into groups of three and choose one person to be hurt. The other two get your chairs ready and put the third person inside. Then you can practice moving around the room.

You might have all groups race from one place to another at the same time, or you may choose to have groups race one at a time with a stopwatch. Or you may choose to just have a couple groups who would like to race.

Discussion points: Heroes often have to know how to handle tough situations. The human chair activity may come in handy someday so you should know how to do it. One thing that makes the human chair activity work is that the people cooperate. Heroes don't always work alone. Many times they lead others to work together. That's what's happening in this activity.

Hero Field Guide

Supplies needed: The Hero Field Guides from the previous lesson and page 83, photocopied and cut for each child, glue, and crayons or markers. For preschoolers you may want to use the Hero Color Sheet on page 82 instead.

Instructions: Glue the Bible verse onto today's page. Decorate as you have time. Be sure to collect the Field Guides at the end of this activity and save them for the next lesson.

Discussion points: Convictions are rules that we have in our hearts. Our Bible verse today comes from a psalm. We're not completely sure who wrote this psalm, but many believe that our hero, David, was the author. The point of the verse is that when we take God's Word and hide it in our hearts it helps us to fight evil, choose right, and be a hero. What are some ways you can hide God's Word in your heart? Memorization, reading it over and over again, writing it out in a journal, etc. Most importantly, the Bible becomes part of you because you allow the truths that it teaches to become convictions in your heart.

What children believe is so important. The scriptures provide the basis for our beliefs. Talk to your children about the scriptures. The Bible stories and lessons from God's Word provide the basis for interaction, decisions, and choices we make. Look for ways every day to bring biblical principles into the daily lives of children. When you do, you'll be accomplishing what Deuteronomy 6:6-7 says, "These commandments that I give you today are to be upon your hearts. Impress them on your children. Talk about them when you sit at home and when you walk along the road, when you lie down and when you get up." The Bible is practical and helps children develop convictions in their own hearts.

✶ ✶ ✶ ✶ ✶

Convictions Game

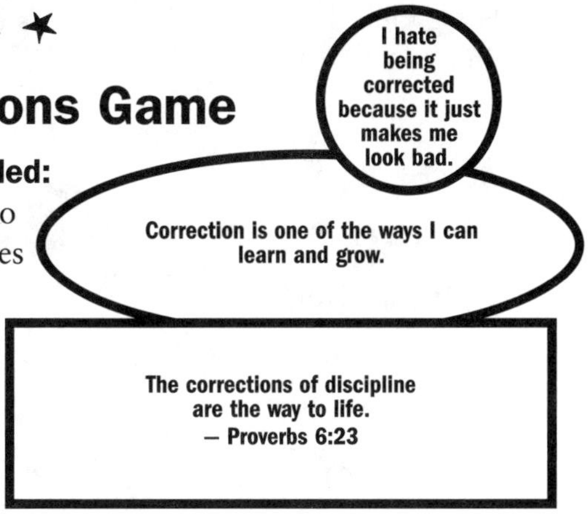
I hate being corrected because it just makes me look bad.
Correction is one of the ways I can learn and grow.
The corrections of discipline are the way to life.
– Proverbs 6:23

Supplies needed: Photocopy onto card stock pages 77 and 78 for each child. You'll also need scissors and small plastic bags to hold the game pieces for the children to take home.

Instructions: You might want to have children work on this activity on the floor to break up the time they'll spend at tables in this lesson. Have children cut out the 15 game pieces and put their names on the top of the game board. This is a matching game that helps children consider thinking errors and their corresponding convictions to keep them on track. Bible verses are also provided to help children think about God's wisdom.

Have children work independently first to try to match up the pieces accordingly. After about five minutes if there are unfinished pieces they can work in pairs or help each other finish the puzzles. When they're done, they can put their pieces in the small bags to save for later. It's fun to get them out and show Mom or Dad and see how long it takes a parent to match them all up.

Note: The order of the rows may differ from child to child. The important thing is that they are correctly matched up in each row.

Discussion points: Heroes have the ability to look past what others normally think and develop convictions that help them do the right thing. The best convictions come from the Bible. In this matching game you're trying to figure out some of the corresponding convictions that will help overcome thinking errors.

To further this exercise you might ask the children, "Can anyone give me an illustration or story of one of the convictions?"

For preschoolers: It's probably best to not do this activity with preschoolers unless you have a lot of time to explain and illustrate the truths.

✶ ✶ ✶ ✶ ✶

Craft

Code Breaker Wheel

The Real Letters
HERO
CODE BREAKER
The Code Letters

Supplies needed: Photocopy the Code Breaker page and the Code Breaker Wheel page on pages 79 and 80, one set for each child. You'll also need a brad for each child and scissors.

Instructions: Have children cut out the Code Breaker circles, poke a small hole in the center of each, and put the brad through the middle. Then the children can use the Code Breaker Wheel to decode the first message on the Code Breaker page and then create their own messages to pass on to someone else. They won't be able to start decoding until you give them the Key Letter (Q for this activity). They will then turn the wheel so that the triangle is pointing to that letter. Then they can match the letters from the inside of the circle on the coded message and decode it by writing the outer letters underneath. When they're done they'll be able to read the message.

Next, children can create their own secret message. The child first turns the wheel so that the triangle is pointing to any letter of their choosing. This letter then becomes the Key Letter for the code. That letter should be placed in the little box in the right hand corner of the big box at the bottom of the page. Next, the child will create a message. That message might be, "Dad I love you." Or "Billy, I think you're cool." Or some other nice comment that will encourage someone. Write the message without the code in the top box. Next, using the corresponding letters put the coded message in the bottom rectangle. After they put the code in the bottom rectangle they can cut out the rectangle and pass it on to their friend with the Code Breaker Wheel.

Discussion points: Heroes often know things that others don't know. In fact, they often believe things that help them to be strong and do what's right. In this activity, you will have a Code Breaker Wheel that will help you to send messages that others won't be able to understand unless they have the Code Breaker Wheel and the Key Letter.

God has given us the Bible. In many ways it's like the Code Breaker Wheel because when we have it and we read it, it makes sense out of life. Sometimes people mistreat us like they mistreated David. Life seems so unfair at times. We feel discouraged and hopeless. Then we read the Bible and we see that God is bigger than the problems we have. He loves us and cares for us. He gives us the ability to forgive or to hang in there even though we feel like quitting. It's like we have the secret code of life that allows us to go on and continue to do what's right.

Convictions are the things we learn from God and believe in our hearts. Those convictions are often the key to helping us deal with the difficulties of life. It is important for you to know what you believe and to have those beliefs based on God's Word.

In this activity you can share words of encouragement with someone else. Create a coded message for someone, maybe your mom or dad or brother or sister, and say something simple and special to them. Watch them break the code and see the delight on their face. You might say, "Mom, I love you" or "Dad, you're great" or "Ralph, I'm glad you're my brother."

For preschoolers: Since this whole activity is based on the ability to read letters, most preschoolers won't be able to do it. Instead, use the maze on page 81. The maze is designed for preschoolers and can help you teach children that there is a right way to complete the maze. In the same way there are right ways to do things in life. For example, when Mom says to do something we do it right away. That's obedience. When you're playing with toys, you share with others. That's being kind. Doing the right thing is important in life.

★ ★ ★ ★ ★

Snack
Trail Mix Buffet

Play the Hero Song (optional) as children are eating their snack. Have a camera ready to take pictures of the children making their own snacks.

Supplies needed:
Raisins, mini pretzels, O-shaped cereal, banana chips, chex cereal, and any other ingredient you would like to add or substitute for one on this list. You'll also need one serving bowl for each ingredient, serving spoons for each ingredient, and a small plastic bag for each child.

Instructions: Put the ingredients in bowls and put the bowls on a table for the buffet. Give each child a plastic bag and tell them that for snack today they will be going through the buffet line and, using the serving spoon, create a mixture of ingredients to put into their plastic bag.

Discussion points: The emphasis in this snack is on the idea of making choices. I want you to be able to choose how much of each ingredient you want to put into your bag. Each one of us makes

choices every day about what we're going to do and how we're going to live our lives. I want you to think about the choices you make this week. Remember, heroes often make different kinds of choices than other people do.

Heroes choose to take initiative and don't wait for someone else to tell them what to do. Heroes admit when they've done something wrong and they look for ways to do what's right. Heroes are honest even under pressure and heroes care about others, not just themselves. As you make choices about life, think about making hero choices based on convictions.

★ ★ ★ ★ ★

HERO Exercise

As you practice at home look for ways to make good choices based on something that you believe. Here are some suggestions you might do, or you may come up with your own. Be ready to report back next time at Hero Training Camp.

- Help someone who is hurting because heroes look out for others' feelings and not just their own.

- Clean up a mess that you didn't make because heroes take action to help out.

- Thank someone for something because heroes appreciate the good that others do.

- Respond right away to parents because heroes are quick to obey.

★ ★ ★ ★ ★

Conclusion

Supplies needed: Compass

Today we've talked about convictions. They are the inner beliefs that help heroes go the right direction. Emotions can lead us along the wrong path so we have to be careful about making decisions based on emotions. Thinking errors or false beliefs about life can also lead us in the wrong direction.

Let me ask you a question. What are the four directions of the earth? One of them is north. What are the others? south, east, and west. Good. Who can tell me which direction is south from here? Does anyone know? Who would like to guess? Someone might say, "Well, there's the door. That must be north." That's a thinking error, right? Just because a door is pointing one way, doesn't make that north. Someone else might say, I feel like that way is north. That would be a mistake because feelings don't always tell us what's right. I have here a compass. Does anyone know how to use this thing? The pin in the middle is pointing north. I have to move the outside of the compass so that the pin is pointing at the N for north. Then I can tell which direction is south or east or west.

In the same way, God's Word is like a compass for us. It gives us truth. We can take those truths and put them into our hearts and then they become convictions. Those convictions then help us know what direction we're supposed to go. God stores those convictions in the conscience. It's important for you to develop convictions in your life and use the Bible to help you know what those convictions ought to be.

SEEING IT THROUGH THE EYES OF A CHILD

Joe says to his sister, "You can't do anything right."

Mom, using a conscience approach says, "Joe, that was hurtful. How do you think someone feels when you make that kind of comment?"

Joe: I don't know.

Mom: I'd like you to go sit down in the hall for a few minutes and then come back when you're ready to talk about this.

Joe, having been gone for 15 minutes, returns: Ok, I'm sorry.

Mom: An apology is good and necessary but why is it important to be kind to your sister?

Joe: I don't know.

Mom: It has to do with a conviction in your heart to be honoring to all people. That's what Romans 12:10 says, "Honor one another above yourself." I'd like you to apologize to your sister and then think of a couple of ways you can honor her right now and report back to me before you're free to go.

Later, after Joe completes his assignment, Mom asks again, "Why is it important to be kind to your sister?"

Joe: Because I'm obeying God by honoring others. It was actually kind of fun to see her happy when I showed honor to her.

★ ★ ★ ★ ★

Prayer

Dear God, thank you for the Bible. Thank you that it gives us the truths we need in order to be heroes. Lord, please help us take those truths and put them into our hearts as convictions so that we too can be heroes for you. In Jesus' name, Amen.

Square Puzzle

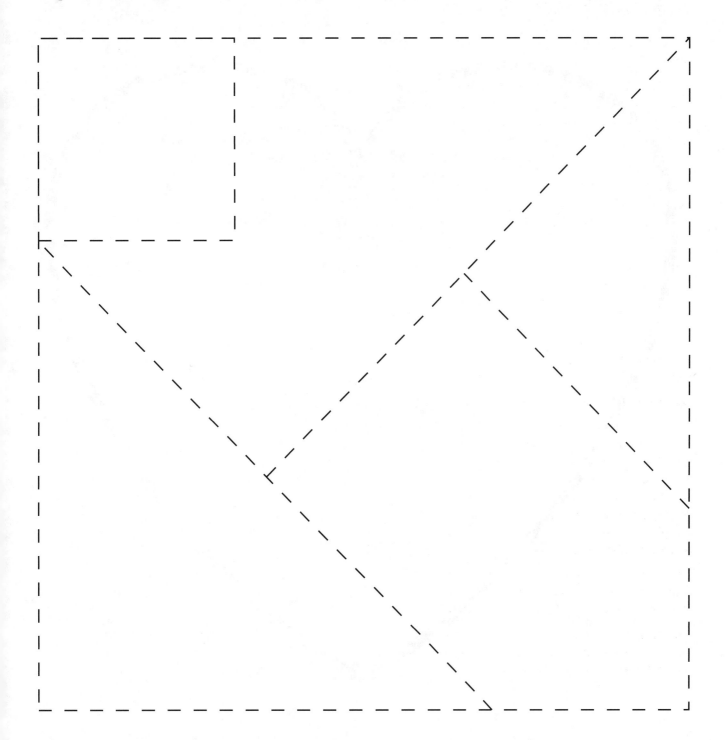

Square Puzzle

Puzzle Game Board (Preschoolers)

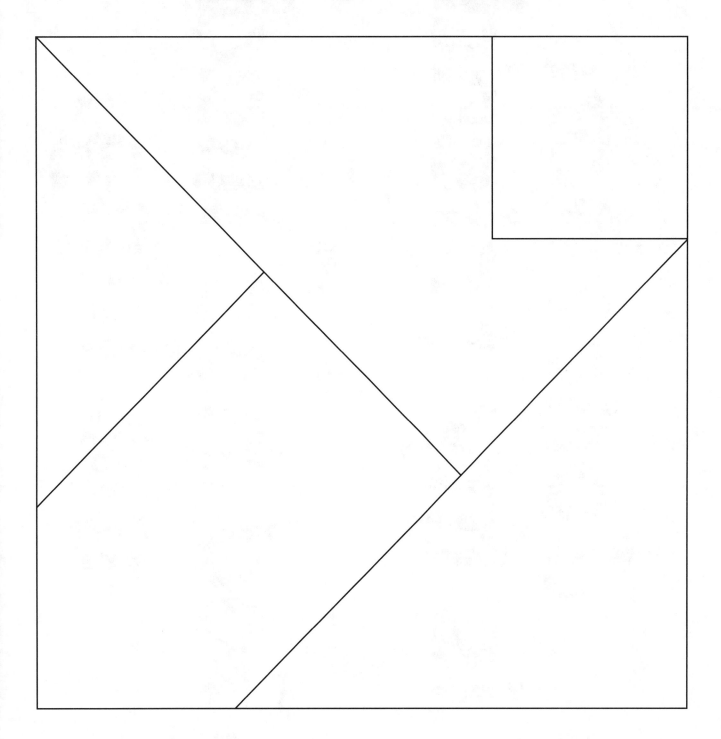

David's Belief #1:

Jonathan is my friend.

David's Belief #2:

God has made me king.

David's Belief #3:

God is in control.

Belief Example #1:

Recycling is important.

Belief Example #2:

Stealing is wrong.

Belief Example #3:

Convictions Matching Game

Instructions: Match the thinking errors on the left with the convictions in the middle and the related Bible verse on the right.

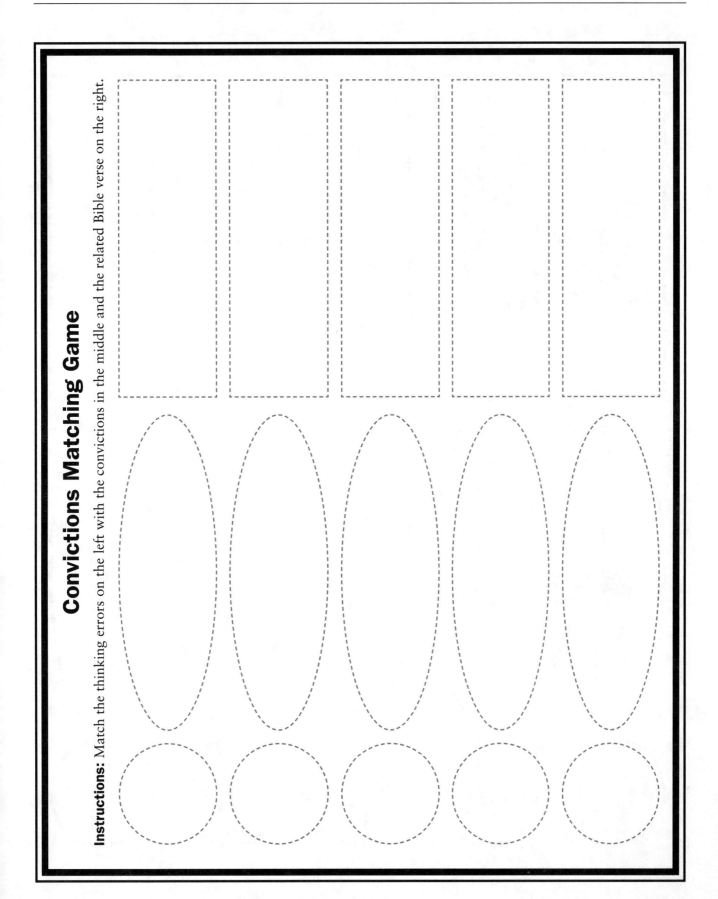

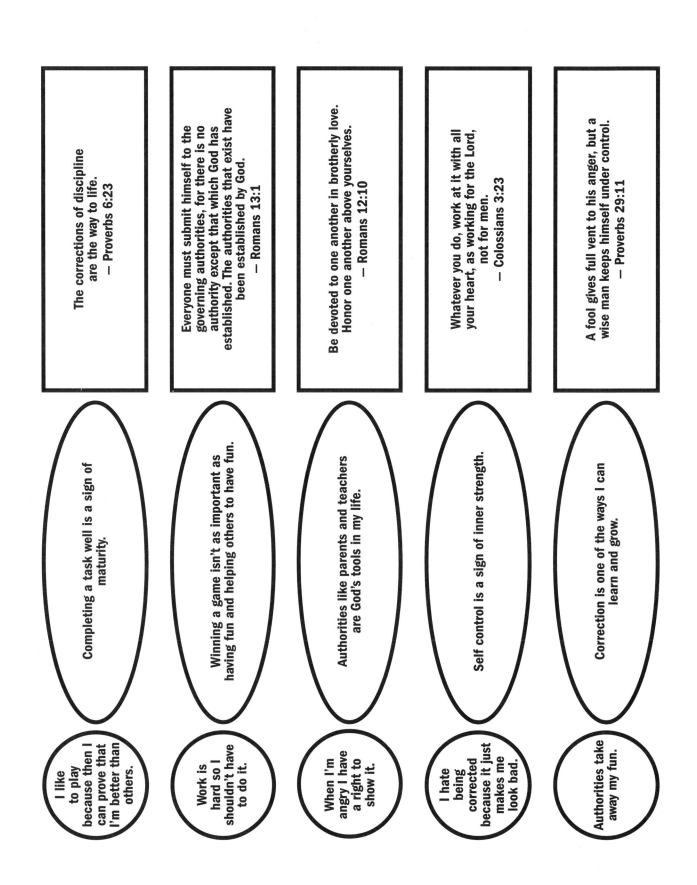

The corrections of discipline are the way to life.
— Proverbs 6:23

Everyone must submit himself to the governing authorities, for there is no authority except that which God has established. The authorities that exist have been established by God.
— Romans 13:1

Be devoted to one another in brotherly love. Honor one another above yourselves.
— Romans 12:10

Whatever you do, work at it with all your heart, as working for the Lord, not for men.
— Colossians 3:23

A fool gives full vent to his anger, but a wise man keeps himself under control.
— Proverbs 29:11

Completing a task well is a sign of maturity.

Winning a game isn't as important as having fun and helping others to have fun.

Authorities like parents and teachers are God's tools in my life.

Self control is a sign of inner strength.

Correction is one of the ways I can learn and grow.

I like to play because then I can prove that I'm better than others.

Work is hard so I shouldn't have to do it.

When I'm angry I have a right to show it.

I hate being corrected because it just makes me look bad.

Authorities take away my fun.

Code Breaker Wheel

Code Breaker Craft

Using your Code Breaker Wheel decode this message:

GLUSZGCZLUO KZSE TE OCIEUKCV

_ _ _ _ _ _ _ _ _ _   _ _ _ _   _ _   _ _ _ _ _ _ _ _

To create your own secret message first write in this space what your message is without the code. Be sure to ask if you need help with spelling.

Using your Code Breaker Wheel, first match up the little triangle with any letter you'd like. Be sure to write down that letter because it's the key to unlocking the code. Put that letter in the small box below. Then find the letters from your message above on the outside of the wheel and put the letter from the inside below. Make sure all of the words have the same amount of letters as they are supposed to as a check for yourself.

Use the Code Breaker Wheel to decode this message.

The students will cut out the bottom box and give it to the person along with the Code Breaker wheel.

Start here

HEROES Know the Right Way to Go

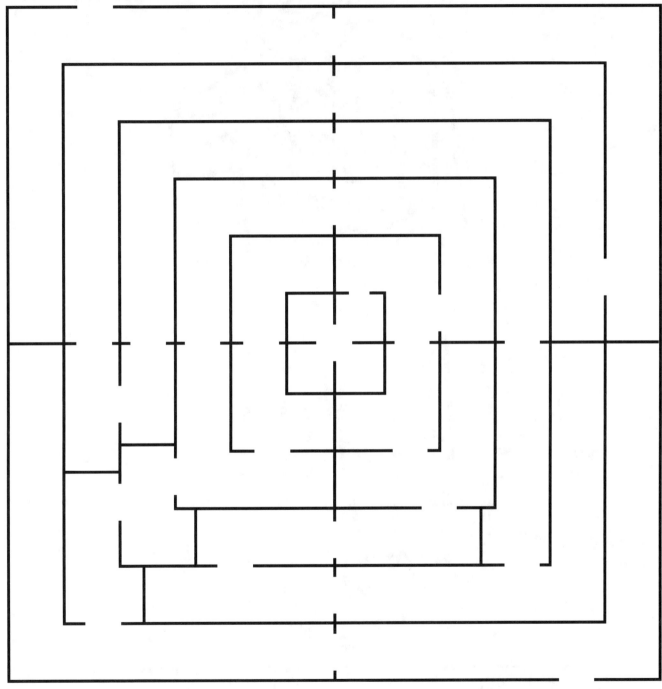

HEROES HAVE CONVICTIONS

I have hidden
your word in my
heart that I
might not sin
against you.

Psalm 119:11

I have hidden
your word in my
heart that I
might not sin
against you.

Psalm 119:11

I have hidden
your word in my
heart that I
might not sin
against you.

Psalm 119:11

I have hidden
your word in my
heart that I
might not sin
against you.

Psalm 119:11

NATIONAL CENTER for BIBLICAL Parenting

76 Hopatcong Drive, Lawrenceville, NJ 08648-4136
(800) 771-8334 or (609) 771-8002
Email: parent@biblicalparenting.org
Web: biblicalparenting.org

Heroes Develop Convictions About Life

Dear Parent,

In our lesson today we learned that heroes make choices based on convictions. We define convictions for kids as the rules in our hearts that tell us what we should do or, beliefs in our hearts that make us do the right thing. All children have convictions already, but some of them are erroneous or just plain wrong. For example, if a child believes that he should be able to get to the next level of his video game before obeying his mother, then his faulty conviction will lead to conflict.

One of the ways you can help your children develop helpful convictions is to use the common rules you have in family life. Each of those rules likely comes from one of your own convictions. If you take some time to explain to your children the values and convictions behind the rules, then your children will have a greater understanding and may be more inclined to embrace those convictions as their own. Convictions are internal rules that govern one's actions.

The **Bible verse** for this lesson is Psalm 119:11, "I have hidden your word in my heart that I might not sin against you." The **Power Words** children can say to themselves are, "I will develop convictions based on God's Word." The children were given a **Hero Exercise** for this lesson to look for ways to make good choices based on something that they believe and be prepared to share that with us next time. This assignment may be a little tough for most children so any help you can give here would be appreciated.

One of the challenges is the temptation to rely on emotion instead of conviction for action. When children choose to react because of a feeling, they are missing an opportunity to respond out of conviction.

The more you talk about and help children understand convictions, the more you are able to help them see that they are making choices in life based on important principles. Talk about the Bible as the greatest source of truth and how convictions can come straight out of God's Word. You'll be surprised at the internal growth you see in your child as a result.

Blessings,

Scott Turansky   Joanne Miller

HEROES Help Others

Preparing Your Heart to Teach Session 4

A significant part of the conscience has to do with caring about others. It motivates people to think about how others feel and looks for ways to help them. In fact, when a person helps someone else, there's a feeling of satisfaction in the heart. That's the conscience at work. Of course, some children are quite weak in this area. In fact, a child may be so mean and insensitive at times, that parents think the child doesn't have a conscience. The reality is that all children have a conscience but some need extensive work to develop it.

One function of the conscience is to prompt children with compassion to care about others. Jesus demonstrated compassion on a number of occasions in contrast to the disciples or the crowds who didn't seem to care (Matthew 9:36, 14:14, 15:32, 20:34).

Thinking about others requires that a person do three things. First, recognize the feelings of another person. Second, be willing to take initiative, and third, become less self-focused. This lesson teaches all three of those areas and provides opportunities for discussions in the various activities. Remember that you're not just trying to get kids to be nice to others, you're trying to help them think differently. Look for ways to identify the mental and spiritual roadblocks that are preventing children from being compassionate toward others.

Supplies Needed for this Lesson

The Pen is Mightier than the Sword
Supplies needed: Photocopy the note cards from page 96, plus pens, art supplies of your choosing, and letter-size envelopes

Making a Penny Shine
Supplies needed: Lemon juice, cup, 2 tarnished pennies, baking soda, and water

The Crippled Race Supplies needed: Two pieces of rope about 3' long

You're the Winner Game Supplies needed:
Photocopy pages 97 and 98. Make two copies of each page for each child so that every student receives a total of four pages. You'll also need scissors and an envelope for each child.

Hero Field Guide
Supplies needed: Hero Field Guides from the last lesson. Also photocopy the verse for today on page 100, plus glue, and crayons or markers

Natural Bird Feeder
Supplies needed: Craft floral wire approximately 18″ long for each child, popcorn, a paper clip, and about 24″ of string per child

Always Room for One More
Supplies needed: Large blankets (one blanket for every 8-10 kids), camera

Creamy Delight
Supplies needed: Non-dairy whipped topping (Cool Whip), vanilla yogurt, raisins, granola, cups, plastic spoons, mixing bowl, and mixing spoon

Other suggested items:
• Photocopy the Parent Letter for each student.
• Have a camera ready to take pictures.
• Be prepared to play the Hero Song if you have the Hero Training Camp Music CD.

Session 4 ★ HEROES Help Others

Theme

Heroes are known for their willingness to help others.

Power Words

I'm always on the lookout to help others.

Theological Truth

God uses the conscience to prompt me to help and bless others by doing more than what's expected.

Welcome Activity
The Pen is Mightier than the Sword

Note: Children may start this activity now but will have time to finish it later during the lesson.

Supplies needed: Photocopy the note cards from page 90, plus pens, art supplies of your choosing, and letter-size envelopes

Instructions: As children are coming have them start working on the Hero Skill Building Activity described on page 83. Those who finish one greeting card can always create another one later in the session.

Discussion points: Sending a greeting card means that you first must think of someone who would benefit from a greeting. Everyone needs encouragement so as you spend a few moments thinking about someone else who needs to be cheered up, you're exercising an important muscle. We call it a compassion muscle. It's not really a muscle like in your arm, but it is in your heart. God wants us to continually look for ways to encourage others and that requires that we think about how other people are feeling.

For preschoolers: This is a fun and meaningful activity for preschoolers. They can color a picture for someone to provide encouragement. Ask the question, "Why did you pick that person?" Try to get children to move outside of themselves to think about the other person's feelings. You might want to write down the child's comments on the card for the person who will receive it.

Together Time

I will LISTEN with my 👁👁, keep my 👄 UNDER CONTROL, Do what the 👩‍🏫 SAYS, knowing that becoming a HERO for God is MY GOAL.

Gather together and remind children of the Hero Training Creed. Take a few moments to help children calm down and prepare their hearts with a prayer, asking God to settle the hearts and provide opportunity to focus on today's training.

Review the Hero Exercise from the previous session. In our last session we talked about making good choices based on what you believe. Can you tell us a time when you were able to do that?

Hero Training Creed:

I will listen with my eyes, keep my mouth under control, do what the teacher says, knowing that becoming a hero for God is my goal.

Introduction
Making a Penny Shine

Supplies needed: Lemon juice, cup, 2 tarnished pennies, baking soda, and water

Instructions: Show the tarnished pennies to the children. Talk about how dull and unattractive they are. Then put one penny into some lemon juice in a cup for about one minute. Take it out and see how shiny the penny is, comparing it to the untreated penny. Pass the pennies around so that children can touch them.

How it works: Pennies are made of copper and normally tarnish in the air. The acid in the lemon juice reacts with the copper, resulting in a shiny penny. Sometimes a minute isn't long enough for the completion of the shine. If it still has a little tarnish on it, you can rub it with a paste of water and baking soda, resulting in a beautiful shiny penny. Of course other stains won't come off a damaged penny with lemon juice but it still illustrates the point.

Discussion points: Today in our lesson we're going to learn how to make other people shine. It's amazing how acts of kindness can bring out the best in other people. They smile and are often kind in return. Heroes are known for their kindness to others. In our lesson today we're going to hear a story about David's kindness in an interesting situation.

★ ★ ★ ★ ★

Bible Story
A Big Act of Kindness

Using the thoughts below and the text from 2 Samuel 4:4 and 2 Samuel 9, tell children the following story. You may have to change the wording or the explanations to match the developmental level of the children you're working with.

Heroes are people who do extraordinary things every day. They share their resources and love or they show incredible strength and courage and inspire others by their

example. In a moment I'm going to share a story about a modern day hero, but before I do I want to tell you another story in the life of David.

After David killed Goliath he was invited into the royal palace of King Saul to play music for him. During that time, David met Saul's son Jonathan and they became great friends. They would play together, talk about life, and they even made an agreement to always be friends and to take care of each other's families.

Many years passed. It was a sad day when David got the word that both Saul and his son Jonathan had died in battle. David was very sad that he lost his best friend Jonathan. Many other people were sad too that Saul and Jonathan were dead. In fact, some people were even afraid that David would kill all of Saul's family because David would be the new king.

Jonathan had a little boy, his name was Mephibosheth. Can you say that name? Mephibosheth. Now this little boy was five years old when his father Jonathan was killed in battle. At the time, he had a nanny taking care of him. And when the nanny heard that Jonathan had died, she was afraid for Mephibosheth, that some soldiers might come and kill him. So she quickly scooped him up to run away and hide.

But a sad thing happened. As she hurried to get out of the house there was an accident. Mephibosheth fell down and hurt his feet.

In those days they didn't have hospitals so poor Mephibosheth's feet never healed properly and he couldn't walk. Other people had to take care of him and help him get from one place to another.

David was very busy after the death of Jonathan and Saul. David had to fight the Philistines and the Jebusites and others. The Bible tells us that God blessed David and gave him victory over his enemies.

After several years David got the new kingdom all set up and the Bible tells us that "David reigned over all Israel, doing what was just and right for all the people." (2 Samuel 8:15)

When things settled down a bit, David missed Jonathan, his friend. David remembered the good times they had together. He had an idea. "I wonder if there is anyone left in Saul and Jonathan's family that I could be kind to?" David didn't know about Mephibosheth.

David called a man named Ziba. He used to be a servant in the house of Saul. Maybe he would know if there was any way that he could help someone in Jonathan's family. "Are you Ziba?" David asked when the man came into the palace.

"Yes," he said.

"I have a question for you. Is there anyone left in Saul's family that I could show kindness to?"

Ziba thought for a moment and said, "Yes. Jonathan had a son and he is crippled in both feet."

David sent for Mephibosheth. I wonder what the young man thought. Would David kill him? Why would the king want to have him come and visit the palace? Maybe Mephibosheth was embarrassed because he couldn't walk and both of his feet were crippled.

When Mephibosheth arrived at the palace, he bowed down to David to pay him honor. David could tell that Mephibosheth was nervous so he said, "Don't be afraid. I want to show kindness to you because your dad was such a good friend of mine. I want to give you land that belonged to your family and I want you to eat here in my palace whenever you'd like."

Wow. That was amazing. Mephibosheth never imagined that he would be eating at the king's table. David was treating him as special. That was a big change for Mephibosheth.

I wonder if people made fun of Mephibosheth because he was crippled. That would be sad, wouldn't it? Sometimes even today people are different on the outside. I know that some children are uncomfortable being around kids that have special needs. Some kids have trouble talking or might be blind or deaf or have to use a wheelchair or walker to get around.

David wasn't bothered by those things. In fact, heroes have an ability to look past the outside of a person to their hearts. Even though a person can't walk or even talk easily, they are still people and

when you get to know them you can look past some of the things that other people see.

David was a hero. But he wasn't a hero just because he killed Goliath. David cared about people. He loved them. He showed kindness. That's one of the things that heroes do. They think about what other people need. Most of the time heroes sacrifice their own desires to help someone else. That's being kind and caring about others.

MODERN-DAY HERO:

IT STARTED AS A KIND GESTURE — but turned into an amazing story. Bill was just ten years old but heard that an older woman at his church didn't have enough money to pay her phone bill. Her phone would soon get turned off. If she lost her phone, her children in other states wouldn't be able to reach her. When he heard the sad story he was touched and wanted to help.

Bill had some money but $74.16 was a huge amount for him. Bill got two of his friends together and asked them to help out too. They liked the idea and together they were able to come up with the amount of money needed. They could hardly wait to give the money to the lady.

Bill's mom contacted the pastor but when they tried to call the woman, her phone was

already turned off. Bill's mom drove the three friends over to the lady's home that evening. Bill told the woman that he and his friends wanted to pay her bill so that she wouldn't lose her phone.

The woman cried and said that they would never know how much it meant to her that strangers would be so kind. She had nowhere to go and didn't know where to turn. Bill explained that they just wanted to help and gave her the money. You would have thought she won a million dollars!

As Bill and his friends left the house, they felt great! The response of the lady was enough thanks for them. They realized that a small act of kindness like that had truly been a great blessing.

God wants us to care about others. That's one of the reasons he's given each of us a conscience. When you see someone who is hurting, you can be the one to care for that person. There's a feeling of compassion on the inside that makes us want to help others who are hurting or sad.

Some people are mean. They don't think about how someone else feels. You don't want to be a mean person because if you are mean on the outside then you are ugly on the inside. God wants us to be kind and compassionate with others. And when you're kind then other people are often grateful. The real reward though is knowing that you've done what's right and that God approves of your kind actions. That feels good!

Take away: God uses the conscience to prompt me to help and bless others by doing more than what's expected.

Bible Verse
Ephesians 4:32
Be kind and compassionate to one another, forgiving each other, just as in Christ God forgave you.

Conscience Insight

The conscience is a prompter but it doesn't guarantee a response. Many children feel sorry for someone or feel a sense of compassion but they don't know what to do about it. Helping children understand people with special needs is an excellent way to help them learn the skills necessary to respond to what they feel inside. When a child sees someone that has some form of handicap or difference, that child may feel put off or afraid. The key is to recognize the things that we have in common. The person may not be able to walk well but he can think just like you. He may not be able to talk as clearly but with a little patience you can still communicate. The conscience prompts children to action but they often need help developing skills to know what to do in challenging situations.

★ ★ ★ ★ ★

Hero Skill Building Activity
The Pen is Mightier than the Sword

Supplies needed: Photocopy the note cards from page 96, plus pens, and art supplies of your choosing, and letter-size envelopes

Instructions: Be sure to cut the note cards as marked so that when folded they fit into an envelope for mailing.

Tell the children to take a moment and think of someone to send a greeting card to, someone who needs to be cheered up or shown some kind of love. This person might be in your family or might be outside your family. It could be a teacher, a friend, a grandparent, or even someone you don't know very well.

Create a greeting card. On the front, in the oval, you might say something like "Thank you" or "To cheer you up today." Or "I love you." Then add another personal statement or draw a picture on the inside. Place the card in the envelope to protect it. (Younger children can draw pictures to cheer the person up or express love.)

Discussion points: Who would like to tell us about the person you chose to send a card to and why? Use the comments of the children to reveal other ways to care about others. Use these kinds of questions to help children feel compassion for others. How do you think the person might be feeling before they receive the card? How do you think the person might feel after they receive the card? How do you think you would feel if you watched the person open the card and they were delighted?

There's a phrase that goes this way, "The pen is mightier than the sword." That phrase came from Edward Bulwer-Lytton in 1839 when he didn't want to fight someone who was attacking him. It is true that writing messages to people is very effective at stopping conflict, providing encouragement, and making others feel valuable.

For preschoolers: Have children color a picture in the card. Write the child's statement on the card to cheer up the recipient.

Role Play
The Crippled Race

Supplies needed: Two pieces of rope about 3′ long

Instructions: We want to have a running race but you won't be able to use your legs. May I have two volunteers? Take the two pieces of rope and tie them each around the ankles of the volunteers. Now I need one more volunteer who will be able to use his legs in this race. The two volunteers

represent being crippled in their legs like Mephibosheth. They must crawl on their bellies and use their arms to move themselves forward and must drag their feet behind them. (Set a starting line and a finish line about 20 feet apart. Be sure to take pictures.)

Get ready to race. On your mark. Get set. Go. The one child who can use his legs can move quickly to the other side. The other two however are crippled. (Remove the rope from the legs of the children.)

Discussion: Mephibosheth was crippled in both feet and he couldn't walk. Do you think he had strong arms to get himself from one place to another? How do you think he might have felt as he moved himself around in life? What about the person who could use his legs to race. How do you think he felt racing against the crippled kids?

Instructions: Now we're going to have another race. We need two more people who won't be able to use their legs (no rope is needed). But we want each of them to have two helpers. Those two helpers hold hands and allow the crippled child to sit between them resting on one set of arms and leaning back on the other. The two helpers then carry the other child across the room.

Discussion: How do you feel as you watch this race? Isn't it fun to see people working together and helping others? Heroes look for ways to do that in life. The illustration in our story is about a boy who grew up crippled, but there are a lot of ways that people are different. Heroes don't look at the differences. Instead they look for ways to help. In fact, some kids laugh at people who are different because they don't understand them or they don't know how to relate well to them. Heroes are willing to look past differences to help others.

★ ★ ★ ★ ★

Game
You're the Winner Game

Supplies needed: Photocopy pages 97 and 98. Make two copies of each page for each child so that every student receives a total of four pages. You'll also need scissors and an envelope for each child.

Instructions: Have the children carefully cut out the cards, providing a total of 2 matching sets of 18 cards, and put them in their envelopes. As a teacher, take some time and play this game with someone else ahead of time, to get the idea of how it's played and to become familiar with the instructions.

How to play the game: Divide children into groups of three. The game can also be played with two players if necessary. Each group only needs one copy of the game (36 cards) so the other

children can put their envelopes with cards aside to take home.

Have one child in each group mix up the cards well and deal five cards to each player. The remaining cards become the draw pile facedown in the middle of the table. Turn over the top card and place it to the side of the draw pile to begin the discard area. The players then pick up their five cards to hold in their hands.

The objective of the game is to show kindness by helping other players get as many pairs as possible.

The player to the left of the dealer starts his turn. This player does one of three things. His choices must happen in this order, and he can only make one move before replenishing his hand from the draw pile, thus ending his turn.

- If he has any pairs in his hand, he must put them down in front of himself. Then draw from the draw pile to replenish his hand and end his turn with five cards in his hand. But if he has no matches in his hand, then,

- He can take a card from his hand that matches any card in the discard area. He takes that pair and gives it to one of the other players, thus demonstrating kindness. He then takes a card from the draw pile to replenish his hand. This ends his turn. If he has no cards to match one in the discard area, he then must,

- Choose one of the cards from his hand and place it in the discard area. He then picks a card from the draw pile to replenish his hand, thus ending his turn.

The next child to the left takes a turn following the same instructions, and play continues from player to player until the draw pile is gone. Then children continue to make moves until all of their cards have been played. You can add to the fun by having the children say, "I want to be kind to you, so I'm giving you this pair" whenever they have the opportunity to give a pair away.

Discussion points: This is an interesting game because the objective of the game is to give the pairs away. In most games you try to collect pairs

Session 4 ★ HEROES Help Others

for yourself to make yourself the best. In this case the rules are different because the objective of the game is to help others be better or to make others happy. That's what kindness is all about. Jesus is the one who said that if you want to be great in my kingdom learn to be the servant of all. This week let's look for ways to be the winner at home by helping others feel good. After all, that's what heroes do. They seek to help others.

For preschoolers: This is a fun game for preschoolers but you'll want to modify it a bit by dealing out all of the cards and having the children place their cards face up in front of themselves instead of holding them in their hands. De-emphasize the rules of the game and taking turns, but instead emphasize matching cards that other people have so that you can help others make matches. In this way you're teaching children to focus on helping others instead of themselves. Talk about how good it feels to help other people.

Hero Field Guide

Supplies needed: Hero Field Guides from the last lesson. Also photocopy the verse for today on page 100, plus glue, and crayons or makers. For preschoolers you may want to use the Hero Color Sheet on page 99 instead.

Instructions: Talk about the Bible verse as you add it to the Field Guide. You might use some of these ideas to help guide the conversation.

Discussion points: The field guide gives us strategies heroes use. One of the things heroes are always looking for is opportunities to help other people. What are some different ways to help others? Be kind, offer comfort, forgive, and take initiative are just a few to mention. Looking for practical examples of these can often help kids catch a vision for putting these principles into practice in their lives.

Craft
Natural Bird Feeder

Supplies needed: Craft floral wire approximately 18″ long for each child, popcorn, a paper clip, and about 24″ of string per child, Hero Song (optional)

Instructions: Mold the wire into the shape of a heart. Before fastening the two ends together, poke the wire through popcorn to fill the wire with the popcorn. Tie one end of the string to the center of the heart and the other end to a paper clip bent into the shape of a hook. Tell children they can take the hanging bird feeders home and hang them on a branch. Play the Hero Song (optional) as children are working.

Discussion points: One way to show kindness is to treat animals well. It usually takes about a week for birds to find a bird feeder once you put it up. You can tie the bird feeder to a tree branch or put it down on a flat surface. Bird feeders attract more than just birds. They often attract squirrels too. That's okay. Squirrels also need food.

Kindness sometimes means that you give to someone when they can't give anything back to you. That's real kindness. But one of the joys of giving is watching others enjoy the gift. That's what happens when you feed the birds or squirrels. It's fun to see them enjoy your gift.

Game
Always Room for One More

Supplies needed: Large blankets (one blanket for every 8-10 kids), camera

Instructions: Spread the blanket on the floor. Explain to the children that this is a teamwork game. The team will work together as a group so that no body parts from any child are touching the ground off the blanket. You can do this as one large group or if your group is too large then you might divide into teams, but make it clear that this isn't a race. (Competition might take the focus off kindness and place it on winning.)

Tell the children that they all need to get everyone from their group onto their blanket. That should be pretty easy because the blanket can easily hold all of the children. If the group completes the task successfully, have them get off and fold the blanket in half and try again. This makes the task a little more challenging, requiring the children to work together. If they are successful, have them get off the blanket and fold it in half again, and then try to get everyone onto the blanket.

Repeat the process for as long as possible. As the blanket continues to be folded in half, the task becomes more difficult requiring creative ideas. As emotions increase the temptation to be harsh increases but also the need to work together builds the team's unity, often revealing consideration to others.

Discussion points: What made this game easy? What made it difficult? Sometimes when people get intense, they stop being kind. One of the keys to kindness is to demonstrate it even when others don't. The real hero isn't the one that leads people to victory. It's the person who can work toward a goal with kindness and encouragement.

★ ★ ★ ★ ★

Snack
Creamy Delight

Supplies needed: Non-dairy whipped topping (Cool Whip), vanilla yogurt, raisins, granola, cups, plastic spoons, mixing bowl, and mixing spoon

Instructions: Allow the whipped topping to thaw in advance. Mix 32 oz of vanilla yogurt with 12 oz of whipped topping in a mixing bowl. Serve the mixture to the children in cups. Allow the children to add raisins and granola to the mixture and

enjoy eating it. This recipe makes 16 half-cup servings. (Fruit works well too if you want to add this as another topping.)

Discussion points: "Has anyone ever had anything like this before? What does it taste like? Some people say it tastes like ice cream. Would you agree? One way to show kindness to others is to share yummy snacks with them." Use the opportunity while children are eating to review some of the things learned today. Ask, "What is the lesson we're trying to learn today?" Allow children to share different ideas. You might follow up with the question, "How might you do that in your family?"

★ ★ ★ ★ ★

HERO
Exercise
Planned Acts of Kindness

As you practice at home, look for ways to show kindness to people. You may plan a way to surprise your mom, make a treat for your brother or sister, or encourage your teacher. Sometimes these acts of kindness come rather spontaneously.

Be on the lookout for opportunities to be helpful, kind, and encouraging to others. Let's try to list some ideas of how we can be heroes by showing kindness unexpectedly. Remember that others may not notice but God does. God loves secret acts of kindness and he always sees what you do even if others don't. Also, you'll feel good in your heart that you did the right thing even if others don't notice.

Session 4 ★ HEROES Help Others

Here are some ideas if kids need help:

- Empty the dishwasher.

- Set the table for dinner.

- Fold the clothes.

- Leave a kind note for someone in a special place like in the kitchen or bathroom.

- Give a hug and say "I love you."

Kindness takes work but it also can be fun. Secret acts of kindness can be even more fun and exciting as you "wait to be discovered." Take advantage of this part of the lesson and you can help children catch a vision for being kind in life as well. The key is to start with the conscience prompter and look for people with needs, emphasizing compassion. Then, ask the question, "Since we see that need, how can we help encourage through kindness." Allow the child to come up with suggestions. This is initiative formation in a child's life. Sometimes you have to help children be reasonable because grandiose plans rarely make it to completion. Then help the child actually do what needs to be done so they can feel a sense of accomplishment. Be sure to debrief afterwards, by emphasizing the conscience again, "How does it feel to do something kind?"

★ ★ ★ ★ ★

Conclusion

This lesson in Hero Training Camp focuses on caring about others. One of the parts of the conscience has to do with thinking about how others feel and caring for those who need help. As you have a final conclusion with the children,

take time to review the lessons learned and emphasize the fact that heroes care about others and think of others' needs, not just their own.

In fact, God has placed a conscience inside each one of us to remind us to think about others, help them, care about their needs, and not be mean or unkind. In addition, God speaks to us and motivates us to help others and sometimes even tells us when and how to do it. So be listening to God and watch for opportunities to help others. Here's a helpful story you might want to tell the children.

SEEING IT THROUGH THE EYES OF A CHILD

An eight-year-old boy was watching through the window of the donut shop. He enjoyed seeing the man make the donuts right there next to the window. He was putting them in the oven and then placing them on display for all to see. The poor boy didn't have any money and his parents couldn't really afford to buy donuts, but he enjoyed watching nonetheless. Just then a man came by and stopped before he entered the store. He was a US Marine and had just returned home on leave. He stood and watched the boy who was obviously lost in the fun of watching the baker. He said to the boy, "Would you like one?"

"Sure," said the boy.

"I'll be right back." The Marine went into the donut shop, bought some donuts, and came out and gave one to the boy.

Wow, the boy couldn't believe his eyes.

He was so pleased and took a small bite, enjoying every moment of this experience. He looked up and saw the Marine walking away. The boy quickly called out, "Hey mister?"

The Marine turned and looked back. "Yes?"

"Are you God?"

It's interesting that when we give to others in special ways without expecting anything in return we are like God. In fact, that's when we become the real heroes of life.

Today you can be like God and be a true hero by looking for ways to help others. I'll be interested to hear about some of your stories.

Prayer

Dear God, we know that a lot of people get frustrated or sad in life and they need encouragement. I pray that you would use our heroes here to be the people who bring hope and kindness to others. Please give them opportunities to show kindness and give them the courage to do what's right. Amen.

HEROES CARE ABOUT OTHERS

Be kind and
compassionate
to one another,
forgiving each
other, just as
in Christ God
forgave you.

Ephesians 4:32

Be kind and
compassionate
to one another,
forgiving each
other, just as
in Christ God
forgave you.

Ephesians 4:32

Be kind and
compassionate
to one another,
forgiving each
other, just as
in Christ God
forgave you.

Ephesians 4:32

Be kind and
compassionate
to one another,
forgiving each
other, just as
in Christ God
forgave you.

Ephesians 4:32

76 Hopatcong Drive, Lawrenceville, NJ 08648-4136
(800) 771-8334 or (609) 771-8002
Email: parent@biblicalparenting.org
Web: biblicalparenting.org

Heroes See What Needs to Be Done and Take Initiative

Dear Parent,

In **Hero Training Camp** children are learning how to take initiative in everyday life. One of the ways to do that is by showing kindness to others. Special emphasis was placed on looking for ways to care about other people and their needs. To reinforce this lesson in your family you might have discussion of times when people have been kind to you, plan a time to partner in kindness to help someone, or even show extra kindness to your child as a way of illustrating this important concept.

Acts of kindness often start with a motivation of compassion. Some children are quite weak in this area and need some work. Spend some time in the coming weeks talking about compassion, how others feel, and requiring an appropriate response. Some children ignore any feelings of compassion and are mean. Those children need more intense work in this area. You might say things like, "How do you think your brother feels when you make that mean comment?" to try to awaken some compassion from within.

Require kindness in the coming days. That may seem hard because you wish that it would just naturally flow from the heart. If it does, great. If not, then sometimes you have to get it flowing by requiring it often. For a child who is particularly mean you might have to say, "I want you to think of three kind things you can do for your sister before you're free to go." Kindness is not optional.

The **Bible verse** for this lesson comes from Ephesians 4:32, "Be kind and compassionate to one another, forgiving each other, just as in Christ God forgave you." The **Power Words** are, "I'm always on the lookout to help others." The **Hero Exercise** for this lesson is to look for secret ways to show kindness. This means that you, as a parent, must be on the lookout to respond with delight to any acts of kindness from your child. It also means that your child may need some help to plan them.

Children often need help taking initiative because initiative takes work. It's one thing to feel sorry for someone. It's another thing to take some action to help.

Practicing the ideas and principles learned in this lesson can help your child develop hero qualities that will be used in your home as well as out with others. But it takes some work and practice to be the kind of person that cares about others.

Blessings,

Scott Turansky

Joanne Miller

God's First Aid Kit

Preparing Your Heart to Teach Session 5

One of the challenges to the conscience is an offense or mistake. When someone does the wrong thing the conscience goes into action, using guilt to prompt repentance. Guilt is actually, a good emotion that assists in the work of gaining a clear conscience. Although the conscience can prompt one to change, it's the Holy Spirit that empowers a person to make changes.

Many children, however, have not yet learned to respond properly to guilt and thus misinterpret its message. Those children imagine that they are inadequate, unworthy, or unloved because of the offense or the mistake.

In this lesson children will explore the area of the conscience that deals with mistakes and offenses. Emphasis is placed on the value of correction, learning from mistakes, and dealing with offenses. The Bible verse, Proverbs 6:23, is a powerful reminder that correction leads to a greater quality of life. Therefore, one's response to correction is very important.

A clear conscience is a treasure. Ultimately, God, through the death of his son, provides forgiveness and salvation for clearing the conscience. Yet even after we become believers we still sin, so we must have an ongoing plan for sin and mistakes in our lives. Children need to learn how to ask for forgiveness from God and from others, learn from their mistakes, and move forward in life.

Read Hebrews 9:9 and then 9:14 to learn an important lesson about the conscience. A clear conscience is one of the benefits provided through the sacrifice of Jesus Christ. We receive forgiveness from God and that clears the conscience. Then we work it out in our lives both with God and with others. Also look at Acts 24:16 where Paul describes his desire to maintain a clear conscience before God and men. The conscience has an ongoing work in a person's life.

As you wrap up this lesson and complete the Hero Training Camp curriculum, look for ways to reflect on the many lessons children have learned throughout. We only remember a little of what we hear or experience. We all need reminders. You can help children remember the key elements of the conscience and motivate them to continue to develop it in their lives.

Supplies Needed for This Lesson

Easier Said than Done
Supplies needed: Paper and pencils for each child, objects to draw such as an orange, a jar, and a small bottle of juice

The Churning Guilty Conscience
Supplies needed: A cup of hot (but not boiling) whole milk, a plate, a few drops of food coloring (red, blue, and green if possible), and liquid dish soap

Bible Story
Supplies needed: A first aid kit with a few basic supplies like bandaids and antibiotic cream

Will You Forgive Me?
Supplies needed: Photocopy the game on pages 115 and 116 for each child, plus scissors, and a small plastic bag for each child

Session 5 ★ God's First Aid Kit

I'm Lost. I Need Some Help.
Supplies needed: A couple of small pieces of chocolate like Hershey kisses, a blindfold

Rebuilding Trust One Step at a Time
Supplies needed: Two sheets of letter-size paper for each child (this paper can be written on, it doesn't have to be new)

Parachute
Supplies needed: Using lightweight plastic trash bags (tall kitchen trash bags work well), precut 16″ square pieces of plastic for each child, plus four pieces of light string or yarn about 16″ long, and penny-size metal washers, two for each child

Bagel Faces
Supplies needed: Sliced bagels (one half bagel for each child), flavored cream cheese, butter, and several vegetables such as carrot sticks, cherry tomatoes, peas, sliced bell peppers, alfalfa sprouts, and sliced cucumbers, plastic knives, plates, and napkins

Hero Field Guide
Supplies needed: The Hero Field Guides from the previous lesson and the verse from page 118 photocopied and cut for each child, glue, and crayons or markers

A Clear Conscience
Supplies needed: Blue liquid food coloring, a clear 16 oz glass with 1 cup of bleach, another clear 16 oz glass with 1 cup of water, two spoons for stirring

Other suggested items:
- Photocopy the Parent Letter for each student.
- If you have the Hero Training Camp Music CD, be prepared to play the Conscience Song in this lesson. You may purchase the Hero Training Camp Music CD at biblicalparenting.org.
- Have a camera ready to take pictures.

Theme

When something is wrong a hero has the courage to fix it, even when he's the one who did the wrong thing.

Power Words

I know the power of admitting when I'm wrong and asking for forgiveness.

Theological Truth

God has a plan for me to respond well to offenses and to grow and learn from them.

Welcome Activity
Easier Said than Done

Supplies needed: Paper and pencils for each child, objects to draw such as an orange, a jar, and a small bottle of juice

Instructions: Provide two or three simple objects on the table and ask the kids to try to draw them on paper. The process of rendering a 3D object on a 2D piece of paper is a challenge for most people. Some children will have a better ability to do this than others.

Discussion points: Drawing an object is not an easy task. Most of us have a hard time drawing anything that is recognizable. Some people won't even try because they're afraid to make a mistake or afraid that others will laugh at their work. But heroes are willing to take the risk because they learn from their mistakes. Heroes know that overcoming problems is one of the ways that we learn and grow.

Today our lesson is about how heroes respond to mistakes and offenses. This is a very important lesson because some kids don't do very well in this area. Some children, when they make a mistake, blame it on others, or get angry with themselves. In this lesson, you'll see the importance of responding well to mistakes and offenses and you'll learn how to do it.

For preschoolers: Young children love to draw. Although they can't draw a three-dimensional object, they can try. Children may get frustrated and want to start over because they made a mistake. It's that moment of seeing a mistake that you can capitalize on in this lesson.

★ ★ ★ ★ ★
Together Time

I will LISTEN with my 👀, keep my mouth UNDER CONTROL. Do what the teacher SAYS, knowing that becoming a HERO for God is MY GOAL.

Gather together and remind children of the Hero Training Creed. Take a few moments to help children calm down and prepare their hearts with a prayer, asking God to settle the hearts and provide opportunity to focus on today's training. Review the Hero Exercise for the previous session. In our last session we talked about ways that heroes help others. Taking initiative to do something kind takes some work. Can anyone tell us when he or she was able to do something kind?

Hero Training Creed:

I will listen with my eyes, keep my mouth under control, do what the teacher says, knowing that becoming a hero for God is my goal.

★ ★ ★ ★ ★

Introduction
The Churning Guilty Conscience

Supplies needed: A cup of hot (but not boiling) whole milk, a plate, a few drops of food coloring (red, blue, and green if possible), and liquid dish soap

Instructions: Pour the hot milk onto the plate as deep as the plate will allow. Put three drops of each color of food coloring into the milk. It's more interesting if you put each color in a different part of the plate, like three points of a triangle. Then drop two drops of liquid soap into or around each color and watch what happens.

How it works: The soap breaks down the fat in the milk, causing the colors to swirl around and churn for several minutes. Hot milk works dramatically because the heat speeds up the chemical reaction.

Discussion points: God has created a conscience inside of each person. That conscience is sensitive to wrongs. When you do the wrong thing, then the conscience prompts you to deal with it and make it right, apologizing or correcting the situation. The Holy Spirit also works in your heart to prompt you to do the right thing. If you don't do what's right, then your conscience churns and churns with guilt and makes you an unhappy person. God has a plan for dealing with offenses in life. In this lesson you'll learn how heroes respond to mistakes and offenses the right way.

God wants you to have peace in your heart, not be churning and upset. God calls that a clear conscience.

★ ★ ★ ★ ★

Bible Story
The Big Mistake

Supplies needed: A first aid kit with a few basic supplies like bandaids and antibiotic cream

This Bible story is taken from 2 Samuel 11-12. Use the Bible and the following thoughts to teach the story and the lesson to the children. You may have to change the wording or explanations to match the developmental level of the children you're working with.

David was a good king and he did what was just and right and fair. People loved him because he obeyed God and cared for the people. Today I want to tell you about a time when David did the wrong thing.

The real test of a hero is the ability to deal with wrongs, even if you caused them. You see, some people, when they make a mistake or do the wrong thing, try to blame others or justify it by saying, "It really wasn't that bad." Or they say, "Other people do worse than that." These kinds of excuses aren't signs of a hero. Let me tell you how David handled a wrong in his life.

One day, King David was up on the roof of his palace looking out over the land. He saw Bathsheba, the wife of one of his soldiers, over at a house nearby. David made a serious mistake that day and decided he would take Bathsheba to be his wife. That was the wrong thing to do. It was stealing. Then, in order to cover it up he sent word to the battlefield to have the armies pull back leaving Uriah, Bathsheba's husband, out in the open where he would get killed. And that's exactly what happened. Now, besides stealing Uriah's wife, David murdered Uriah.

> I HAVE SINNED AGAINST THE LORD.

That was bad. But David thought he could cover it all up. He couldn't. Bathsheba became pregnant and had a baby. It was at that time that Nathan the prophet came to visit David. Nathan made up a story to trick David. Here's the story he told.

There were two men in a certain town. One was rich and the other was poor. The rich man had a very large number of sheep and cattle, but the poor man had nothing except one little lamb he had bought. He raised that lamb and it grew up with him and his kids. The lamb shared the man's food, drank from his cup, and even slept in his arms. It was like a daughter to him. The lamb was his precious pet.

One day the rich man had a guest come and he wanted to cook the guest a nice dinner. But instead of going to get one of his own sheep for the meal he went and took the special lamb from the poor man, killed it, and cooked it up for dinner.

Nathan told that story to David. How do you think David might have felt when he heard that story? Angry, wanting to go out and get the guy and put him in jail or something, right?

The Bible tells us that David burned with anger. He was very upset. He told Nathan, "This man deserves to die. He must pay back the poor man four times as much because he didn't care about the poor man but was just being selfish."

Nathan then said, "David, you're the man. God gave you so many things. He took care of you when you were running away from Saul. He gave you a family of your own and you are now the king over Israel. But you were selfish and you killed Uriah and took his wife to be your own."

David felt terrible. But instead of blaming or making up excuses he did the right thing. He said, "I have sinned against the Lord."

Because David confessed that he had done the wrong thing, Nathan said, "OK, David, because you have confessed you will not die. But there are consequences to your sin. The baby that your wife Bathsheba had will die."

David was so sad. He loved that little baby. So he cried and sat with the baby for a whole week before the baby died. It's a sad story. Whenever we do the wrong thing there are consequences. Sometimes the consequences come from parents or teachers, but the worst consequence is the one inside. You know you've done the wrong thing. The guilt from doing wrong is the worst consequence of all.

The interesting thing is that God doesn't want us to live with guilt. Guilt is a prompter that says, "You should make it right. Go apologize. Go confess. Get rid of your guilt." Even when you do confess, often there is a consequence but in your heart you know that God has forgiven you and you are not hiding your sin anymore. Guilt is a terrible thing to live with and God has designed a plan for dealing with it.

I like to think of God's plan for mistakes and offenses as a First Aid Kit. I have one here and see the things that are in it? Bandaids, gauze, pain reliever, antibiotic cream. We use the first aid kit when we have some kind of injury. It helps in the healing process. God has created a First Aid Kit for our hearts. It has several pieces in it. We'll learn more about some of those things in this lesson. But the result is that we experience forgiveness. We end up with a clear conscience. That's healing for the heart. And it's a great experience to know that you have a clear conscience.

David wrote a song after he was forgiven. We don't have the tune but here are the words. Listen to the joy in David's heart when he was forgiven, compared to the guilt of trying to cover up his sin.

Psalm 32:1-5

Blessed is he whose transgressions are forgiven, whose sins are covered. Blessed is the man whose sin the LORD does not count against him and in whose spirit is no deceit.

When I kept silent, my bones wasted away through my groaning all day long. For day and night your hand was heavy upon me; my strength was sapped as in the heat of summer.

Then I acknowledged my sin to you and did not cover up my iniquity. I said, "I will confess my transgressions to the LORD" and you forgave the guilt of my sin.

Forgiveness is a beautiful thing and it starts with confession and asking for forgiveness. That's one of the signs of a hero. The story of David and Bathsheba doesn't end there. It continues on because it wasn't long before David and Bathsheba had another baby on the way.

God sent the prophet Nathan to David again. What would he say about this new baby? Nathan came and said, "You can name the baby Jedidiah, which means loved of the Lord."

Wow, isn't it great that God forgives? It's like God was saying to David, "It's okay now. We dealt with the sin. We need to put the problem behind us. You can go ahead and grow your family and build the kingdom I've called you to build." Isn't God good? He forgives.

We all make mistakes. Sometimes they are bad ones, sometimes small ones, but how we respond to those mistakes is very important and reveals a lot about our hearts. Some kids blame themselves and say, "I'm such an idiot. I'm never going to get it right. People don't like me. I don't even like me." Other children say, "It's okay. It's not that bad" or "It's not my fault, it's somebody else's fault." These are not the right responses to mistakes. The solution is to confess and get forgiveness. Those are tools in the First Aid Kit.

That's God's way.

God is so great. He even uses our mistakes to help us grow. We can learn from them and he often then uses our mistakes to help us help other people too. One of the important characteristics of a hero is that heroes are able to deal with their own mistakes. Our wrongs are often opportunities for us to learn to do the right thing, trust God, or do better next time.

Session 5 ★ God's First Aid Kit

But that requires a special attitude toward mistakes and offenses. Think about the last time you made a mistake or did the wrong thing. Did you try to cover it up and hide it? Did you try to blame it on someone else? Did you try to justify it and say it really wasn't that bad? Don't do that because then you miss the benefit of learning from your mistakes.

God wants us to learn from our mistakes. It starts with confession and admitting that we've done the wrong thing. That often requires more courage than fighting an enemy. But you're in Hero Training Camp and heroes must learn to fight all kinds of battles, even the ones that are inside our hearts.

Take away: God has a plan for me to respond well to offenses and to grow and learn from them.

For preschoolers: Emphasize the part of the story that talks about David's response to sin. Young children need to learn how to deal with their offenses. This story illustrates what children need to do. They must confess and ask forgiveness. That simple concept is valuable for preschoolers to understand.

Bible Verse
Proverbs 6:23
The corrections of discipline are the way to life.

The Conscience Song

If you have the Hero Training Camp Music CD this is a good place to introduce the Conscience Song.

Supplies needed: Hero Training Camp Music CD

Instructions: Play the Conscience Song and ask children, "What is this song trying to teach us?"

Discussion points: Some of the ideas you might want to reinforce are, "Jesus is working inside of us." "Temptations are an opportunity to listen to God in our lives." "We all experience temptations and they come in various ways."

Conscience Insight
Mistakes often trip children up when it comes to apologies and making things right. After all, sometimes a child unintentionally hurts someone else. The temptation is to say, "I didn't do anything wrong so I don't have to apologize."

The reality is that the child may not have done anything morally wrong, but accidentally hurt another child. That mistake or accident, although innocent, still leaves an offense. The way to deal with offenses is to go to the other person and apologize. An apology not only addresses wrongs committed intentionally, but it also provides relational healing for the mistakes or accidents we have in life as well. God has provided a way to obtain a clear conscience for things you didn't even mean to do and that is to seek forgiveness.

Hero Skill Building Activity
Will You Forgive Me?

Supplies needed: Photocopy the game on pages 115 and 116 for each child, plus scissors, and a small plastic bag for each child

Instructions: Have the children cut out the game pieces and put them in their plastic bags. Take pictures of children playing this game to use later.

How to play the game: Pair up the children. You'll only need one game set to play with, so one child from each pair can put a game set aside. While one child turns around, the other child arranges the board so that all the pieces are upside down except for

the four forgiveness cards. They are kept off the board. This is a matching game, so the child who turns away will be choosing two cards at a time, trying to find a match.

Explain to the children that there are several different kinds of offenses one might commit. Some affect people while others are just between you and God. Some of them are intentional. Others are called mistakes because you didn't intend to do them. Some of them are sin and others don't involve sin. (See below for examples if you want to elaborate or have a deeper conversation about sin and offenses.)

In this game we'll focus on mistakes of two different kinds. One kind involves other people and the other kind doesn't. It's important to know how to handle both of them. If it's just a mistake like when you trip over the carpet, then you can learn from that. If it involves another person, such as bumping into someone in the hall, then you need to apologize. In both cases they were unintentional so they were mistakes.

Your goal in this game is to turn over game pieces that match. If you turn over two pieces that don't match then that represents a simple mistake that doesn't require an apology but is an opportunity for you to learn something. In that case you'll simply say, "Oops, I made a mistake. I can learn from that."

In addition, there are four OUCH! cards on the board. Those cards represent the times when you made a mistake that hurt someone else somehow and you need to apologize, even though you didn't mean to offend the other person. When you turn over one of those cards that has the word "OUCH!" written on it, then you say these words, "Oops, I made a mistake. Will you forgive me?"

The other person then gives the player a forgiveness card and says, "Yes, I forgive you." And the game continues. The one child continues his turn

until he has revealed all of the cards. If there's time, have the children reverse roles and play again.

Discussion points: Heroes know how to handle mistakes, sin, and offenses. It's helpful to know the difference. A mistake is something you do that's accidental. You didn't mean to do it. Some of those involve other people and some of them don't. What's an example of a mistake that involves someone else? You pick up the wrong backpack thinking it was yours until the person points it out. You forget to take your pajamas out of the bathroom and your brother goes into the bathroom and your clothes are on the floor. What is an example of a mistake that doesn't involve someone else? You add wrong and come up with the wrong answer. You leave your pajamas in the bathroom but find them yourself before anyone else does.

Sometimes we do things that aren't mistakes. They are intentional. We mean to do them. Sometimes those things might affect other people as well. For example, you might get angry with your friend and yell at him. That's the wrong way to handle a problem. Many times the wrong things we do, not only hurt others, but they are called sin because they violate God's standard. When we sin, we also need to talk to God and ask his forgiveness as well. Other examples of sin might be ignoring your mother when she calls you or asks you to do something. Or being selfish and leaving a mess that you know you should clean up.

God has a plan for all kinds of mistakes, sins, and offenses. As soon as you make a mistake or have an offense, you want to deal with it. God has created a plan to deal with these problems. Confess and ask forgiveness. That's what this game helps to remind you to do. Once you practice these kinds of statements in the game then you can say them in life. When you make a simple mistake that doesn't involve someone else, then say to yourself, "Oops, I made a mistake. I can learn from that." And when you make a mistake that does involve someone else, say to them, "Oops, I made a mistake. Will you forgive me?" If what you did wasn't a mistake, be sure to ask God to forgive you and, if someone else is involved, ask that person to forgive you as well. Then you can keep a clear conscience before God and man.

Parents know that praise is important. However, many parents overemphasize forms of praise that focus on parental approval. These are statements that say things like, "I like that," "I'm pleased," or "You did a good job." These comments essentially say to a child, "You make me happy," and are external prompters. Although these kinds of comments aren't wrong and children do need to know that you admire and appreciate them, another form of praise is also important and is often lacking in parental vocabulary. This is the kind of praise that focuses on affirming the child's initiative and character, and affirms the internal prompters like the conscience or God's work in a child's heart. "It must feel good to be growing up," "You're going to make a great dad someday with that kind of thoughtfulness," "It looks like you feel pretty good when you do the right thing."

In the above game for example, when a child figures out two pieces that match, say, "How does that make you feel?" It feels good. "Yes, it feels good when you do the right thing." Over and over again in this activity children are repeating statements. You too can reinforce the concepts taught in this lesson.

Role Play
I'm Lost. I Need Some Help.

Supplies needed: A couple of small pieces of chocolate like Hershey kisses, a blindfold

Instructions:
Sometimes knowing the right thing to do is not easy. Life can get pretty complicated. This game reminds us of the importance of asking for help. Show children a piece of candy and tell them you are going to put that candy somewhere in the room, maybe on the floor behind the door, on a window ledge, or in a cup on the counter. Then you'll choose one person to be blindfolded who will find the candy by

I'M LOST. I NEED SOME HELP.

following the instructions of others. Instructions can only be given one at a time and only when the child says, "I'm lost. I need some help." Take pictures of children giving instructions to the "lost child."

Ask for a volunteer to be blindfolded. This can be frightening for some, so be sensitive and make sure the child feels okay once the blindfold is on. Make a trip around the room and as you do, deposit the candy in a place that others see and continue walking around the room so that the blindfolded child doesn't kno3w where you actually deposited the candy. Then say, "OK, you can begin." The child needs to say, "I'm lost. I need some help." Upon that cue, the leader points to someone else in the room who can give an instruction such as, "Take three steps forward," or "turn left," or "reach your hand out." Only offer one directive at a time and then remain silent until the child again says, "I'm lost. I need some help." In this way, the group is leading the child to the candy, but the child is initiating and asking for help.

Discussion points: A hero doesn't always have the answers. But heroes know where to find answers. When you don't know what the right thing is to do, who might you go to for advice? Parents, teachers, friends, family members. Don't forget, we can always pray too. James 1:5 tells us that if we lack wisdom we can ask God and he'll give us help. Heroes know how to ask for help in the right places.

Game
Rebuilding Trust One Step at a Time

Supplies needed: Two sheets of letter-size paper for each child (this paper can be written on, it doesn't have to be new)

Instructions: Give each child two sheets of paper. The assignment is to stand at one wall and make it to the other wall by stepping only on the paper you have in your hands. As you take one step you put another piece of paper down and so on in order to make it to the other side. If you fall off the path you have to pick up the paper and start over. This isn't a race. This is just to see if you can make it to the other side.

Although there's no competition built into this activity, some children will want to be first. The self-created pressure often results in mistakes that have the person start over again. If that happens you can use that example in your debriefing. This is a fun activity for picture taking.

Discussion points: When a person does the wrong thing, they often lose the trust of others. It takes some work to rebuild that trust. In this game, we can imagine that the first wall represents a time when you did the wrong thing and you have to prove that you can do what's right again. Sometimes that's called being responsible or being trustworthy. It takes time to rebuild that trust. And it happens one step at a time. If you make another mistake or do something wrong then that's represented in the game by falling off the paper. You often have to start all over to rebuild trust again.

That's why it's so important to do what's right. When you do the wrong thing, you need to make it right as quickly as possible. If you try to cover it up and hide it, or make excuses, then you're just doing more wrong things and breaking trust some more. By admitting you did the wrong thing and asking for forgiveness, you're helping to rebuild trust.

Craft
Parachute

Supplies needed: Using lightweight plastic trash bags (tall kitchen trash bags work well), precut 16″ square pieces of plastic for each child, plus four pieces of light string or yarn about 16″ long, and penny-size metal washers, two for each child. It would be good to test out this particular craft to make sure that the weight of the washers is right for the parachute. To test, take it outside and throw it up in the air. The goal is to have it unfold and float down slowly. The thickness of the plastic, the even length of all the strings, and the weight of the washers all play an important role in getting the parachute to work.

Instructions: Have the children tie one piece of string to each corner of the plastic. Then take the four loose ends of string and tie them together onto the two washers (the washers stack on each other, using two to provide the weight needed). After making the parachute, pinch the center of the plastic, allowing the strings and washers to hang down. Gently fold the plastic in thirds from top to bottom and wrap the string lightly around the folded parachute. Throw it up in the air and watch it float down slowly. (If you didn't fold it too tightly, it should unfold, catch in the air, and float down gently.) You may want to go outside to get the full benefit of watching them float through the air. Be sure to take pictures of children catching their parachutes.

Discussion points: While children are making the parachutes, talk to them about the conscience. Use this activity time as an opportunity to review some of the lessons of the previous sessions. In the same way that the parachute has four corners, the conscience has four parts. Do you remember what they are? Do what's right, deal with wrongs, be honest, and care about others.

Those four parts of the conscience are all important. What if you were to try to fly the parachute with only three strings instead of four? It would just fall to the ground and crash. The same thing is true with your life. You need to have a strong conscience in all four areas. If there's an area that's weak, you better work on it. If you have a hard time with honesty, it's time to change. If you struggle with being kind and caring about others, working on this area of your life is important.

For preschoolers: Most preschoolers will not be able to tie the knots necessary to make a parachute. You can eliminate this activity or make the parachutes ahead of time. The preschoolers will enjoy playing with them. You might talk about how parachutes can protect heroes from danger, just like a strong heart can help us to do the right thing.

★ ★ ★ ★ ★

Snack
Bagel Faces

Supplies needed: Sliced bagels (one half bagel for each child), flavored cream cheese, butter, and several vegetables such as carrot sticks, cherry tomatoes, peas, sliced bell peppers, alfalfa sprouts, and sliced cucumbers, plastic knives, plates, and napkins

Instructions: Give each child a half of a bagel. Have the children spread cream cheese or butter on the bagel and then arrange the vegetable pieces to create a face. Take pictures of the bagel faces next to the child's own face just for fun.

Discussion points: Use the opportunity to review some of the lessons learned from the activities today. Remind children that heroes deal with offenses and mistakes. They have the courage to deal with their own mistakes, not just help others correct wrongs. Talk about forgiveness and how important it is for a clear conscience and how valuable a clear conscience is for life.

★ ★ ★ ★ ★

Hero Field Guide

Supplies needed: The Hero Field Guides made in the previous lesson and the verse from page 118 photocopied and cut for each child, glue, and crayons or markers. For prescoolers you may want to use the Hero Color Sheet on page 117 instead.

Instructions: Give children their Hero Field Guides and talk about the Bible verse as you add it to the next page of the guide. You might use some of these ideas to help guide the conversation.

Discussion points: The Bible verse today reminds us that correction and discipline help us learn and grow. There are a lot of ways to learn something. You can learn by watching someone else on a video or by listening to a teacher. You can read a book or do an experiment. Those are all ways to learn. Another way that we can learn something is through correction. Some people are afraid of correction. They believe it's a sign of weakness, something to be avoided. A hero learns from correction and recognizes that correction and discipline are great ways to help us be more successful in life.

HERO Exercise

Look for a way to apologize or admit you were wrong. Remember that an apology is a sign of strength, not weakness.

SEEING IT THROUGH THE EYES OF A CHILD

Several children were asked what it means to be forgiven or to be done with a discipline; here are some of their responses. Notice their sense of a clear conscience.

— **I feel like it's over, and I'm free to go.**

— **It's the same feeling I have when school's out and I get to go home.**

— **I just want to take a deep breath.**

— **I'm sad that I did the wrong thing but I know that my smile will come back soon.**

— **I feel like my mom and I are friends again.**

Conclusion
A Clear Conscience

Supplies needed: Blue liquid food coloring, a clear 16 oz glass with 1 cup of bleach, another clear 16 oz glass with 1 cup of water, two spoons for stirring

Instructions: As you talk through the discussion points below, put two drops of blue food coloring in the glass of water and two drops in the glass of bleach. Stir them both up and watch what happens.

How it works: Bleach contains chlorine which produces hydrochloric acid and atomic oxygen. Food coloring contains chromophores that reveal color. The oxygen reacts with the chromophores to eliminate the portion of its structure that causes the color, making the color disappear.

Discussion points: At the beginning of this lesson today we put some food coloring representing offenses into the milk along with some soap and we saw some churning. That's a good picture of what happens with a guilty conscience. Here's another illustration. The food coloring makes the water all colored, but when we drop the offenses into the bleach, then the conscience knows how to get rid of them. Do you remember the ways that we can deal with mistakes and offenses? Admit what we did wrong, apologize, and learn from it. God has a plan he wants us to use for dealing with sin, mistakes, and offenses. When we follow God's plan, we can have a clear conscience.

One of the biggest challenges we all must overcome in order to be a hero is to deal with ourselves first. You have to deal with the enemy inside you in order to be a hero. That enemy is

sin. Sin often tempts us to be selfish and do the wrong thing or to be too tired to do the right thing, or to take the easy way out and lie, or to not have the courage to deal with offenses.

God has given each person a conscience to help us feel stronger and at peace when we've done what's right and uncomfortable when we've done something wrong. Furthermore, God places his Holy Spirit inside us to do those same things — and even more. The Holy Spirit not only indicates an offense, but also gives us the power to overcome it. No matter what you have going on inside of you that might be keeping you from becoming a hero, God can change you. In fact, that's what he loves doing. God loves changing people from the inside out.

At this point pour all of the contents from the bleach glass into the glass with blue water and watch what happens. When you have God at work in your heart then he empowers you to do what's right. It starts by asking Jesus Christ to come into your heart. When you have Jesus living inside of you, then you can be a hero every day. God wants to do a work inside your heart. None of us can be heroes on our own. We need the power of God to make that happen. And God gives that power to us freely. If you've never asked Jesus to come into your heart, today's a good day to do it. In my prayer maybe you would like to pray with me to ask Jesus to come into your heart. If so, just say those same words to God and ask him to run your life.

Prayer

Dear God, we are so grateful that you have provided us with a conscience to help prompt us to do right and avoid wrong. Thank you. We also thank you that you want to live inside of us. Lord, I ask that you would work in the life of each child here. We love you. We thank you that you sent Jesus to die on a cross for our sins. I know that I'm a sinner and I want to ask you to come and live in my heart. Lord, I pray that each child here will make that prayer his or her own. In Jesus' name, Amen.

You may want to end the prayer by asking the children to keep their heads bowed and eyes closed and to raise their hands if they prayed that prayer to ask Jesus into their hearts. This will allow you to follow up in ways that nurture their faith.

The Forgiveness Game

WILL YOU FORGIVE ME?

HEROES DEAL
WITH WRONGS

The
corrections
of discipline
are the way
to life.

Proverbs 6:23

The
corrections
of discipline
are the way
to life.

Proverbs 6:23

The
corrections
of discipline
are the way
to life.

Proverbs 6:23

The
corrections
of discipline
are the way
to life.

Proverbs 6:23

NATIONAL CENTER
for BIBLICAL
Parenting

76 Hopatcong Drive, Lawrenceville, NJ 08648-4136
(800) 771-8334 or (609) 771-8002
Email: parent@biblicalparenting.org
Web: biblicalparenting.org

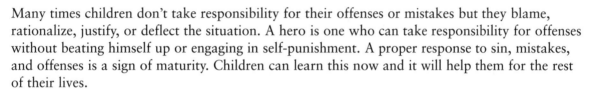

Heroes Know How to Deal with Wrongs

Dear Parent,

Heroes are known for their ability to address wrongs in life. Most of the time we think of those wrongs in others, but the reality is that we have to work inside first. In **Hero Training Camp** today we talked about how God has designed confession and forgiveness as tools for addressing our mistakes and offenses.

Many times children don't take responsibility for their offenses or mistakes but they blame, rationalize, justify, or deflect the situation. A hero is one who can take responsibility for offenses without beating himself up or engaging in self-punishment. A proper response to sin, mistakes, and offenses is a sign of maturity. Children can learn this now and it will help them for the rest of their lives.

The **Bible verse** in this lesson is particularly helpful. Proverbs 6:23 says, "The corrections of discipline are the way to life." The point of the verse is that there is great value found in correction and discipline. It's one of the ways that we learn. A healthy attitude toward correction is important for children but it's also important for parents.

Many parents view correction as an interruption in life. Instead, it would be better to see it as an opportunity for teaching. Parents are often on the treadmill of life, getting things done, and accomplishing the business of family life. When a child creates an offense or makes a mistake, time is needed for correction to take place. If not prepared, parents may experience anger as their activity has to slow a bit to do the work of parenting.

One suggestion is that you plan margin into your life so that you have adequate time and energy for correction. By building margin into your life, you will not be so taken off guard and will be able to respond to the correction task with more patience, wisdom, and vision.

Correction and discipline are actually positive activities. Your attitude is important when children make mistakes because kids catch your attitude. They need to know that mistakes are part of life. We learn from them and move on. Use the tools of confession, apology, and forgiveness to help your children grow in this area of the conscience.

The **Power Words** for this lesson are, "I know the power of admitting when I'm wrong and asking for forgiveness." The **Hero Exercise** for this lesson is to use the Hero Field Guides that they've been creating as reminders to be a hero every day.

Look for reminders and talk to children about the things they've learned at Hero Training Camp. Work spent in this area of developing a sensitivity to the conscience and the Holy Spirit can go a long way to help your child become responsible, mature, and responsive to God.

Blessings,

Scott Turansky

Joanne Miller

Handling the Pressure

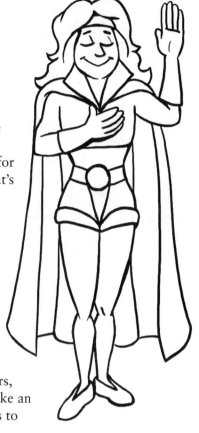

Preparing Your Heart to Teach Session 6

A significant challenge for the conscience is honesty. Interestingly, dishonesty always occurs under pressure. Sometimes it's the pressure to avoid punishment, or to exaggerate a story to impress some friends, or steal to obtain something and satisfy a desire. Those pressures exist all around and the ability to withstand the pressure lies in God's grace and a strong conscience.

In this lesson, you'll help children understand that God-given inner strength can help them handle the pressure of dishonesty. In fact, heroes have the ability to be honest even when it's tough.

You'll also help children understand the long-term benefits of telling the truth. Although dishonesty may provide immediate benefit, honesty always wins in the end, in part because of the satisfaction of a clear conscience.

Paul says in Romans 9:1, "I speak the truth in Christ, I am not lying, my conscience confirms it in the Holy Spirit." He ties the conscience to honesty. Children know when they have been dishonest; guilt and fear are a natural response to their poor choice.

Some children struggle with dishonesty more than others. This lesson will help both those who easily give in to the temptations to be dishonest and also those who aren't as tempted in this area. Most of all, this lesson teaches children about pleasing God with their integrity and thus preserving something that's extremely important for their lives.

Supplies Needed for This Lesson

A Careful Balance
Supplies needed: A helium balloon with a ribbon or string, temporarily secured to a table or chair, paper clips, heavy paper or card stock, and scissors

Put Yourself into the Story
Supplies needed: Photocopy the three story cards on page 131. Just one copy for the teacher is all that's needed.

Amazing Under Pressure
Supplies needed: One large hardcover book for each team (each book should weigh about 2-3 pounds), photocopy paper (20# weight), scissors, rulers, and tape; make an example of supports to show the children

Hidden Consequences
Supplies needed: Photocopy pages 132-140. You'll also need 6 letter size envelopes, glue, and masking tape. (If working with preschoolers, use the color page on page 140 instead.)

Delicious Under Pressure
Supplies needed: Make the Pressure Bars according to the recipe in this lesson. Have them ready to serve the children.

Don't Get Sucked In
Supplies needed: One medium hard-boiled egg (peeled), a little oil, matches, and a glass bottle or jar with a $1\frac{1}{2}''$ opening (a Starbucks Frappuccino bottle works well)

Honesty Badge
Supplies needed: Photocopy page 141 so that each child has one badge. Purchase enough 1" ribbon so that each child can have two 4" strips. You'll also need scissors, glue, and markers along with any other art-related supplies that you think might make the craft experience more enjoyable.

Session 6 ★ Handling the Pressure

Hero Field Guide
Supplies needed: The Hero Field Guides from the previous lesson and page 143, photocopied and cut for each child, glue, and crayons or markers

The Weight of a Guilty Conscience
Supplies needed: One piece of photocopy paper and an unopened ream of photocopy paper

Other suggested items:
- Photocopy the Parent Letter for each student.
- Be prepared to play the Hero Song if you have the Hero Training Camp Music CD.
- Have a camera ready to take pictures.

Theme

Heroes have the ability to be honest even under pressure.

Power Words

I can be honest even when it's hard.

Theological Truth

My integrity is a valuable tool, not only for my conscience, but also for building relationships with others.

Welcome Activity
Hero Field Guides

This is a good time to decorate or fill in any missing pages in the Hero Field Guides for the first sessions. Children who missed one or more lessons can mount the pages in their guide so that they are caught up with the others. Children who are caught up can begin this lesson's Field Guide page.

Supplies needed: The Hero Field Guides from the previous lesson and page 143, photocopied and cut for each child, glue, and crayons or markers

Instructions: Have children decorate or fill in missing pieces from the first lessons.

Discussion points: Heroes are characterized by four distinct qualities. They do what's right, deal with wrongs, are honest, and they care about others. You might talk about contemporary heroes and see how they match up in these four areas. One of the interesting things about today's heroes is that they often have internal issues that they must overcome in order to be heroes. The battle within is a significant battle that must be fought by heroes today.

Although heroes may struggle in areas, their personal integrity along the way reveals their inner strength.

Together Time

Gather together and remind the children of the Hero Training Creed. Take a few moments to help children calm down and prepare their hearts with a prayer, asking God to settle the hearts and provide opportunity to focus on today's training. Review the Hero Exercise that the children were assigned in the previous lesson. In our last lesson we talked about apologizing or admitting you were wrong. Can you tell us a time when you were able to do that?

Hero Training Creed:
I will listen with my eyes, keep my mouth under control, do what the teacher says, knowing that becoming a hero for God is my goal.

Introduction
A Careful Balance

Supplies needed: A helium balloon with a ribbon or string, temporarily secured to a table or chair,

paper clips, heavy paper or card stock, and scissors

Instructions: Take the helium balloon and untie the string from the chair. Using a piece of card stock and paper clips, find the balance point that prevents it from flying up in the air but keeps it hovering over the table. With the children offering suggestions and even helping out, cut pieces off the cardboard or add paper clips as necessary. Take a picture of the balloon in balance to use later. Be sure to include pictures of children next to the balloon.

Discussion points: As we continue to learn about the conscience, we're going to focus on honesty. Today we're going to talk about the life of David, and in our story we'll see that Saul began to let his emotions get out of control. David, on the other hand, was able to keep his desires in check.

This balloon has forces pulling on it. The one force pulls it up in the air. What is that force? The helium inside the balloon. The other force pulls it down to the ground. What is that force? Gravity. There may be other forces in the room such as the air blowing through the vents or wind coming in a window. The challenge is to not let the forces pull the balloon too far in one direction or another but instead to create a balanced state.

People also have forces pushing on them. Sometimes they want to look good to others. Sometimes they're trying to get out of trouble. Some of those forces might tempt a person to use dishonesty. The conscience helps by reminding us that dishonesty is the wrong choice and that we should choose a better response. Heroes can handle the pressure. Today, we'll see how David was able to manage it.

✶ ✶ ✶ ✶ ✶

Bible Story
The Real Test

This Bible story is taken from 1 Samuel 23-24. Use the Bible and the following thoughts to teach the story and the lesson to the children. You may have to change the wording or explanations to match the developmental level of the children you're working with.

King Saul was jealous of David because he knew that David would be king in his place someday. David knew how to obey the Lord and listen to him. Saul was so angry with David that he wanted to hunt him down and kill him. David had to run for his life.

It wasn't long before others heard that David was on the run. In fact, about 600 men joined David's little army. David often asked God about what he should do, and God had David and his men go on missions to help the Israelites. They would fight against the Philistines and other enemies to protect Israel. All the while they had to be very careful because as soon as Saul heard where they were, he would send his army after them to catch them.

David continued to serve the Lord and do the right thing even though Saul was after him.

David could have fought with Saul and his army but he didn't. In fact, David could have been worried about becoming king over Israel. After all, God had promised that he would be king but things didn't seem to be working out the easy way. David understood that God was in charge and that he had a plan. David knew that when the right time came he would be placed on the throne in Saul's place.

Saul sent spies to find out where David was. Several times Saul was on his way to kill David and his men when God helped David escape just in time. One time David and his men were running away from Saul in the desert of Maon. David and his men were moving quickly around one side of a mountain while Saul and his men were coming around just behind, closing in to capture them. Saul's soldiers were getting closer and closer and Saul thought he would capture David this time. But just then a messenger came to Saul and said, "Come quickly! The Philistines are raiding the land."

Saul broke off the chase just in time and David and his men escaped again. God was protecting David. After Saul left, David and his men went over and lived in a place called the strongholds of En Gedi. There were many places to hide, with caves and paths through the mountains that would make it more difficult for Saul to capture David.

But Saul wouldn't stop pursuing David. He was so angry and jealous he wanted to kill David, so this time he took 3,000 men with him to try to hunt David down. Saul's army was looking all over the area for David but couldn't find him because David had found a great place to hide. He and his men went into a large cave and went way back into it. Surely Saul wouldn't find them in there.

It wasn't long though before David and his men heard noise outside the cave. It was Saul and his men. They were going by the cave, hunting for David. Just then Saul had to go to the bathroom. He told his men to go on and he decided to go into the cave to do his

business. Can you imagine? It was the same large cave where David and his men were. David and his men were very quiet. No one moved.

Saul came into the cave, took off his robe, and put it on a large rock. Then he went further back into the cave where he thought he had some privacy to go to the bathroom. It must have been a different part of the cave because David's men had an idea. They said, "David, now's your chance. Go and kill Saul. He's all alone. God has given him into your hands. You can kill him now and then you can be king."

David snuck up to the front of the cave. He saw Saul's robe lying there on the rock. He took out his knife and cut off a corner of the robe and then snuck back to be with the others. At that point, the Bible tells us something very important happened. As David began thinking about killing King Saul, he realized that doing so would be the wrong thing to do. In fact, it would be like cheating. God had a plan and God already told David that he would make him king. David's conscience helped him to realize that he shouldn't kill Saul but that he should let God take care of Saul instead.

Up until now, David had just trusted the Lord and let God do the rest. There was no point doing something different now. David was very interested in doing what's right. He was honest, just, and fair, even when others treated him unkindly. That's one of the things that made him a hero. A hero knows that sometimes the best thing to do is not to fight but to let God work out the problem another way. Sometimes people cheat because they won't wait, or they aren't happy with what they have. David knew that cheating was wrong and he decided he would not do the wrong thing.

Just then, Saul came back out, picked up his robe, and put it on, not realizing that part of his robe had been cut off. Saul headed out of the cave to catch up to his men. As Saul left the cave and began walking down the path, he was stopped in his tracks by a voice. It was David.

David came to the entrance of the cave, bowed down in respect, and said, "King Saul. Why do you listen to people who tell you that I'm trying to kill you? I'm not trying to harm you at all. See?" And David held up the piece of Saul's robe. "I could have killed you today in the cave. In fact, some of my men encouraged me to kill you, but I won't do that. Why are you hunting me down as if I'm a dog? I won't harm you. God will judge between you and me."

David used an interesting strategy. He just spoke the truth. It's interesting how honesty can be such a good strategy. It's true that honesty isn't easy sometimes. In fact, dishonesty always happens under pressure. Stealing, cheating, or lying all happen when a person feels pressure of one kind or another. Sometimes people lie because they want people to like them. Other times they lie to get out of trouble. Still others lie to get something they want. It takes a hero to be honest under pressure.

How do you think Saul felt at that moment? He felt guilty, grateful, surprised. In fact, it's interesting that his conscience started bothering him. The way David responded to Saul allowed God to work in Saul's heart. Saul began to cry because he knew that he had done the wrong thing. He said, "David, you're a better man than I am. You had opportunity to kill me this day and didn't do it. You have treated me well but I have treated you badly."

Saul took his men away and they stopped hunting David. David was a hero, and heroes know how to solve problems without fighting or lying.

Take away: My integrity is a valuable tool, not only for my conscience, but also for building relationships with others.

Bible Verse
Colossians 3:9
Do not lie to each other, since you have taken off your old self with its practices.

★ ★ ★ ★ ★

Role Play
Put Yourself into the Story

Supplies needed: Photocopy the three story cards on page 131. Just one copy for the teacher is all that's needed.

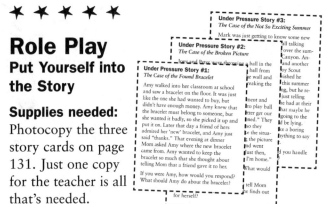

Instructions: It takes courage to tell the truth. I have a story that puts a child in a difficult position. Lying would be an easy way out. Your job is to figure out how to respond in the story without being dishonest. Read one scenario at a time and choose a child to answer the question as if in the situation. If time permits, you might allow another child to respond.

Discussion points: After the situational role plays, debrief with the children about the experience. You might say, "People often lie because it seems like the easy way out. Lying always takes place under pressure. Being honest requires a person to be strong on the inside. Think about times that you are tempted to lie. Whenever you lie, you have given up under pressure. A hero is a person who is able to be strong and do the right thing even when it's tough."

Session 6 ★ Handling the Pressure

★ ★ ★ ★ ★

Activity
Amazing Under Pressure

Supplies needed: one large hardcover book for each team (each book should weigh about 2-3 pounds), photocopy paper (20# weight), scissors, rulers, and tape; make an example of supports to show the children

Instructions: Divide into teams of three, with each team working on a solid surface, either a sturdy table or an uncarpeted floor. Give each team one piece of photocopy paper, scissors, and tape. Give the children the following instructions. "Paper isn't very strong. It wouldn't normally hold up a heavy book like you have in your supplies. But if the paper is cut and shaped a particular way, then it can be strong enough to hold the pressure of the book. Your mission is to use the paper to create stands that will hold the book two inches off the surface of the table or floor. Some people make cylinders and others make star shapes (hold up examples). See what you can do to support the book up off the surface."

How it works: Photocopy paper has a rigidity to it that allows it to withstand the pressure. Folding it or making a cylinder increases its strength because each fold creates a point of support. If you have time, the children might want to experiment with the number of folds. The cylinder has a similar effect because the curve of the paper gives it more support.

Discussion points: Dishonesty can reveal itself in different ways. Some people lie, steal, cheat, or are mischievous like writing on a wall or destroying property when no one is watching. The person who is dishonest is weak on the inside. If you look at our Bible verse for today, you can see that the Bible tells us lying is wrong. It's sad to see someone who is so weak on the inside that they are dishonest.

Honesty is foundational to relationships. If someone is dishonest then you can't rely on that person. Imagine that you have a job to do. You need a person to collect money for tickets as people enter the door. Would you choose someone who is dishonest? No. What if you're a parent and a child wants to stay at home while you run to the store. Would you allow that child to do so if he were dishonest? No. What if you were a teacher and you needed a helper to run an errand to the office. Would you choose someone who was dishonest? No.

Someone who is dishonest is unreliable. In this activity, the book represents a challenging situation. The paper is like a person. The person who is honest can be relied upon to do the right thing even when tempted. Children who are honest don't have to have someone watching them every moment to make sure they are doing the right thing.

Sometimes it's hard to be honest. But in the end, it's the honest person who is trustworthy and reliable and can hold up under pressure. Furthermore, when you're honest, you can feel good in your conscience because you've done the right thing.

For preschoolers: With young children you'll want to tell them exactly what to do. They can help cut the paper and fold it in a way that will support the book. Talk about the amazing strength of a piece of paper when it has the right folds. In the same way a child can be strong under the pressure to be dishonest by having the right strength in the heart.

★ ★ ★ ★ ★

Activity
Hidden Consequences

Supplies needed: Photocopy pages 132-140. You'll also need 6 letter size envelopes, glue, and masking tape.

Instructions: Cut out the 3 Situation Title Cards and 3 Situation Description Cards. Cut out the 6 Choice Cards and glue them each to an envelope. Cut out the 12 Consequence Cards and insert them into the appropriate envelopes. Set up the room with three different situation centers. This will get the children up and moving between each situation. Each situation may take place against a different wall or in a different room.

Tell the children that we will be in the Hero Situation Room today preparing to solve some difficult problems. Let's all get up and go over to that wall over there, sit down on the floor, and I'll give you further instructions when we're ready.

Go to the first wall and pull out Situation Title Card #1; tape it to the wall. Read Situation #1 to the children. After you read the situation, tell the children that we have two possible solutions and put the two envelopes on the wall (each envelope contains two Consequence Cards). Have the children help you tape the envelopes to the wall and help read the Consequence Cards if they are able.

After discussion, go to the next situation room or area and proceed with Situation #2 and then Situation #3 in a similar way.

Discussion points: Notice that there are short-term consequences to each choice and long-term consequences to each choice. When evaluating each situation, help the children recognize all of the possible consequences. Then ask, "Which choice would you make?" This is an interesting question because most of the children will likely respond the way you want them to respond by making the honest choice. However, there's usually someone who will say, "I'd keep the money." To

that person you want to say something like, "Yes, it's very tempting to do the wrong thing and keep the money, isn't it? But what is the right thing to do? Not what would you do, but what is the right thing?" This kind of dialogue further reinforces the idea that there are long-term benefits to being honest.

When you get all done, go back to your main area and ask the question, "What do we learn from this activity?" Of course, children are learning that there are consequences to their actions. Sometimes you can get an immediate solution that seems like a good idea but it has long-term negative consequences. Honesty is hard sometimes but it pays off in the end with some very positive benefits, the most important of which is a clear conscience.

For preschoolers: Rather than working through this activity with young children, you may simply want to discuss honesty while the children work on the Hero Color Sheet from page 142.

★ ★ ★ ★ ★

Snack
Delicious Under Pressure

Supplies needed:
Make Pressure Bars according to the following recipe. Have them ready to serve the children.

6 tbsp of butter
6 cups of mini-marshmallows (10.5 oz bag)
7 cups of puffed corn cereal (round like Kix)
2 cups diced dried fruit (i.e. raisins, cranberries, or chopped apricots)

Butter a 9″x13″ baking pan. In a large pot melt butter and mini-marshmallows over low heat (about 5 minutes). Remove the mixture from the stove and use a wooden spoon to stir in cereal and fruit. Pour the mixture into the 9″x13″ baking pan. Using a slightly buttered metal spatula, press down the treats into the pan and cool in the refrigerator. Cut into bars and serve. This recipe makes 24 bars.

Discussion points: These bars were created under pressure. When the person made them they used a flat spatula and pressed them down into shape. They held up pretty well, didn't they? Heroes can stand the pressure. What are we learning about heroes today? Use the answers to talk about the importance of honesty, building a good reputation, becoming trustworthy, and having a clear conscience.

Children who have a problem with honesty often have other underlying issues that must be addressed. For example, children who lie take shortcuts. They are often unwilling to do the hard work of telling the truth. It's like seeing a sign that says, "Keep off the Grass." Kids may cut across the grass anyway because it's easier. When children lie, they take shortcuts and cut across their conscience. These children often need to learn how to work harder. Many times children who lie are also lazy, looking for the easy way out. One of the ways that you can help children grow in honesty is by teaching them to work hard. More chores and lots of practice are often necessary to build the internal qualities required to work hard. Those same qualities that enable a person to work hard are used to be honest.

Hero Skill Building Activity
Don't Get Sucked In

Supplies needed: One medium hard-boiled egg (peeled), a little oil, matches, and a glass bottle or jar with a $1^1/2''$ opening (a Starbucks Frappuccino bottle works well)

Instructions: Put a little oil around the mouth of the bottle and on the egg. Light a match, drop it into the bottle, and quickly put the egg on top of the bottle, pointed side down. Watch what happens. Take pictures of children watching the egg before and after it drops into the bottle.

How it works: The fire inside the bottle burns up the oxygen, creating a vacuum inside the bottle. If the egg has a good seal on the top of the bottle then it gets sucked in. Because the egg has some flexibility it is able to conform to the bottle opening without breaking.

Discussion points: It's important for heroes to be careful where they spend their time. If a person isn't careful, then the people they hang out with or the places they go can suck them into dishonesty. A hero can see the danger ahead and stays away from dishonest situations.

Ron said to his friend Charlie, "Hey Charlie, let's take this candy bar while no one is looking." Charlie said, "No. It costs too much." Ron said, "What do you mean, it would be free." If you were Charlie, how would you explain to Ron the cost?

It's important for heroes to develop the skill of seeing danger. Watch out for those places that can suck you in to doing the wrong thing. Be prepared to see the consequences of your actions and choose wisely the friends and activities you get involve in.

Conscience Insight

One of the greatest losses experienced with dishonesty is that the child loses the benefit of the doubt. It's a gift generally given to children until they prove to be untrustworthy.

After a child lies or is found to be sneaky, then parents question most other behaviors. The spiral continues when a questionable action is perceived to be dishonest, and the child then feels hurt because he was not doing the wrong thing in that instance. But that is the consequence of losing the benefit of the doubt. People will suppose you're doing the wrong thing instead of thinking that you're doing what's right. The benefit of the doubt is a privilege, that when lost, is hard to get back.

✶ ✶ ✶ ✶ ✶

Craft
Honesty Badge

Supplies needed: Photocopy page 141 so that each child has one badge. Purchase enough 1˝ ribbon so that each child can have two 4˝ strips. You'll also need scissors, glue, and markers along with any other art-related supplies that you think might make the craft experience more enjoyable.

Instructions: Have each child cut out the badge and decorate it. Cut the ribbon into 4˝ lengths and glue them on the back of the badge at an angle. Take pictures of children holding up their badges. Play the Hero Song as children are working (optional).

Discussion points: Dishonesty always occurs under pressure. What are some of the pressures kids might face that tempt them to be dishonest? Or, if kids are having trouble with that question you might simply ask, "Why do some kids lie?" or "Why do some kids steal or cheat?" Use the answers to the questions to talk about the pressure and how a hero can do the right thing even when it's tough.

✶ ✶ ✶ ✶ ✶

Hero Field Guide

Supplies needed: The Hero Field Guides from the previous lesson and page 143, photocopied and cut for each child, glue, and crayons or markers

Instructions: Glue the Bible verse onto today's page. Decorate as you have time. Be sure to collect the Hero Field Guides at the end of this activity and save them for the next session.

Discussion points: Talk about the Bible verse as you add it to the next page of the guide. You might use some of these ideas to help guide the conversation. Why do you think God hates lying? It ruins relationships. People can't trust each other. God is all about truth. Dishonesty is a lack of trust. Help children understand that lying isn't just a bad idea. It's something that violates God's standard of right and wrong.

✶ ✶ ✶ ✶ ✶

 **Exercise**

As you practice at home look for ways to show honesty under pressure. Your assignment is to come back next time with an example when you saw, either in yourself or in others, the pressure to be dishonest. Maybe you can even tell us a time when you saw the pressure there but you chose to do the right thing.

★ ★ ★ ★ ★

Conclusion
The Weight of a Guilty Conscience

Supplies needed: One piece of photocopy paper and an unopened ream of photocopy paper

Instructions: Ask for a volunteer to put their hands out in front of them and hold one piece of paper on their open palms. After a brief discussion have the same child hold a ream of paper on their open palms. It's hard to hold up under the weight of the paper. Take a picture of the child straining under the weight.

Discussion points: Sometimes people think that a little lie won't hurt. After all, it's just like this piece of paper, not a problem to hold up. But then, they lie more and more. This ream of paper contains 500 pieces of paper. The person who starts lying develops a pattern of lying. In fact, when someone catches that person lying, then that person has to lie again to cover up the lies. Pretty soon, the problem is so big that the person has a major problem. The solution is to not lie in the first place. The person who lies goes around with a heavy conscience, always wondering if someone is going to discover the dishonesty. Telling the truth and being honest not only make you reliable before others, but being honest allows you to feel good on the inside as well.

Work on being a hero in the area of honesty. It's an important part of your training.

SEEING IT THROUGH THE EYES OF A CHILD

"I don't know why I lie. I guess I'm afraid of something. When I finally tell the truth I feel better. It's like I'm done. I like feeling done."

– Becky, age

★ ★ ★ ★ ★

Prayer

Dear God, I pray that you would help each of these children make wise choices when it comes to honesty. I pray that you would help them see the pressure coming and have the internal ability that you provide to withstand the pressure. Lord, make each one of these children reliable and trustworthy. We thank you for this important lesson. In Jesus' name, Amen.

Under Pressure Role Plays
Put Yourself into the Story

Instructions: Photocopy this page and cut out the cards. Read one scenario at a time and choose a child to answer the question as if in the situation. If time permits, you might allow another child to respond.

Under Pressure Story #2:
The Case of the Broken Picture

Joey and Peter were throwing a ball in the house. As Joey tried to grab the ball from Peter, his arm accidentally hit the wall and a picture fell to the ground, breaking the glass in the frame.

Mom was due home at any moment and she had often told the boys not to play ball in the house. Peter said, "We better get our story straight about what happened." They didn't want to get into trouble, so they tried to figure out a way to make the situation not look so bad. They hung the picture back up, cleaned up the glass, and went into the backyard to discuss it. Just then, they heard Mom say, "Hi boys, I'm home."

Imagine you are Joey or Peter. What would you do?

Why is it important for them to tell Mom about the broken glass before she finds out for herself?

Under Pressure Story #1:
The Case of the Found Bracelet

Amy walked into her classroom at school and saw a bracelet on the floor. It was just like the one she had wanted to buy, but didn't have enough money. Amy knew that the bracelet must belong to someone, but she wanted it badly, so she picked it up and put it on. Later that day a friend of hers admired her 'new' bracelet, and Amy just said "thanks." That evening at dinner Mom asked Amy where the new bracelet came from. Amy wanted to keep the bracelet so much that she thought about telling Mom that a friend gave it to her.

If you were Amy, how would you respond? What should Amy do about the bracelet?

Under Pressure Story #3:
The Case of the Not So Exciting Summer

Mark was just getting to know some new friends in school. They were all talking about the fun things they did over the summer. One went to the Grand Canyon. Another went to Disney World, and another boy went camping with his Boy Scout troop. As Mark listened, he wished he would have gone somewhere this summer or had done something exciting, but he really didn't. His neighbor was just telling him yesterday about the fun he had at their beach house. Mark thought that maybe he could make up a story about going to the beach, but realized that would be lying. Mark doesn't want to look like a boring guy. He really doesn't have anything to say that's good about his summer.

If you were Mark, how would you handle this experience without lying?

The Case of Too Much Change

(The opportunity to buy the video game you've been saving for)

The Case of the Difficult Test

(An easy way to get the right answers)

Situation #3:
The Case of the Weeds in the Flowerbed
(The fast way to work and get on to playing)

Situation #1 Description
The Case of Too Much Change

Joey went to the store to buy some gum. He gave the cashier a $10 bill but the cashier thought it was a $20 bill and gave Joey an extra $10 change. Joey walked away from the counter and looked at the change and realized that he had too much. Joey knows that the extra $10 would be just what he needs to buy that new video game from the video game store next door. Joey headed for the door but then stopped. He had to make an important decision. What should he do?

Situation #2 Description
The Case of the Difficult Test

Mindy studied for the test but when she got to class, she realized that the questions weren't the same things that she had studied. She didn't know the answers. The teacher had stepped out of the room, and as she looked up she saw that she could easily see the answers on the paper of the boy next to her. He was smart and was always getting A's in everything. Now she knew that she could get the right answers and get a good grade on the test too. She paused for a moment to think. She had an important decision to make.

Situation #3 Description
The Case of the Weeds in the Flowerbed

Josh had a job to do. Dad had asked him to weed the flowerbed in front of the house. Although the flowerbed wasn't too big, there were a lot of weeds that needed to be removed. Dad had explained to Josh that the key to getting the weeds out for good was to pull out the roots. That takes a little more time but it removes them for good. Otherwise, if you just pull off the tops then they grow back. Josh is in a hurry to go play ball with his friends. Josh could just pull the tops off the weeds. No one would notice. The flowerbed would look clean and he could get to the ball game faster. Josh had an important choice to make.

Keep the Money

Return the Money to the Cashier

Copy the Answers from the Boy

Do the Best She Can Without Cheating

Pull the Tops Off the Weeds

Dig Out the Roots

Short Term Consequence

"Wow! This is great," Joey thought. "This is just the amount I need to buy the video game that I saw on sale this week. The cashier's mistake is his problem and my gain." Joey quickly goes next door to the video store and buys the game and takes it home to try it out.

Long Term Consequence

Joey knows the money really isn't his. He starts to feel guilty that he kept the money. Joey wonders what will happen to the cashier when his boss finds out that he comes up short at the end of the day. Every time Joey plays the video game he feels bad because he knows he got it in a way that wasn't right.

Short Term Consequence

Honesty Wins: When given the extra change, Joey turns around and points it out to the cashier and gives him the money back. As he leaves the store Joey thinks about how he might have used that $10 to get the video game on sale this week.

Long Term Consequence

Joey feels good because he did the right thing. Although Joey will have to wait to get the video game, he knows that being honest is worth it because he has a clear conscience.

Short Term Consequence

"This will be easy," Mindy thinks. "I won't get caught because the teacher has left the room. I can easily see the answers. Now I'll be able to get a good grade on this test." Mindy goes ahead and writes down the answers from the boy's paper.

Long Term Consequence

Mindy turns in her test, confident that she'll get a good grade, but then the fears start up. Her thoughts race, "I wonder if the boy had the right answers? I wonder if we were taking different tests? I wonder if the teacher might have been watching through the window? I wonder if anyone saw me cheating?" Fears continue on and they start to affect the way Mindy interacts with the teacher. The teacher calls Mindy's name and she immediately thinks she's caught. Mindy realizes that cheating wasn't worth it.

Short Term Consequence

Honesty Wins: Mindy keeps her eyes on her own paper, does the best she can, and turns in her test. The teacher grades it and, it's true, Mindy got a low grade. She feels bad for the low grade but determines to do better next time.

Long Term Consequence

Mindy knows she did the right thing. Although she got a bad grade, she knows that she was being honest and has peace of mind. Having a clear conscience gives Mindy freedom to not live in fear.

Short Term Consequence

Dad won't be able to tell whether the roots are gone or not. Josh just pulls off the tops and it all looks cleaned out. It doesn't take long for him to rip off all the tops. That job didn't take much work and Josh gets to the ball game just in time.

Long Term Consequence

Josh knows that he didn't do a good job like his dad had expected. Those weeds will grow up in no time. It will become obvious that Josh didn't do a good job. Josh has been wanting to prove to his parents that he is becoming more responsible. This will cause them to question that. Even though Josh gets to play ball, he doesn't enjoy it as much because he feels guilty for not doing a thorough job.

Short Term Consequence

Honesty Wins: Josh did the hard work of digging out the roots, completing the job just the way Dad taught him to. Josh can see the boys playing ball and is eager to get to the game, but he knows that doing this job is important so Josh hangs in there and eventually gets to the game late.

Long Term Consequence

The job is done. The weeds and their roots are out, and Josh feels good. Every time he walks by that flowerbed he feels a sense of accomplishment that he made that flowerbed look nice. Josh still gets to play part of the game, and he feels good inside that he did the right thing.

Craft
Honesty Badge

Do not lie
to each other,
since you have
taken off your
old self with its
practices.

Colossians 3:9

Do not lie
to each other,
since you have
taken off your
old self with its
practices.

Colossians 3:9

Do not lie
to each other,
since you have
taken off your
old self with its
practices.

Colossians 3:9

Do not lie
to each other,
since you have
taken off your
old self with its
practices.

Colossians 3:9

NATIONAL CENTER for BIBLICAL Parenting

76 Hopatcong Drive, Lawrenceville, NJ 08648-4136
(800) 771-8334 or (609) 771-8002
Email: parent@biblicalparenting.org
Web: biblicalparenting.org

Heroes are Honest Under Pressure

Dear Parent,

One very important part of the conscience deals with honesty. But telling the truth or avoiding deception can be a challenge at times. There are several ways that you can teach children about honesty, but none is more valuable than a good example.

One mom said it this way, "As I evaluated my own interaction with my children, I realized that I was exaggerating sometimes or coloring the truth in order to persuade my kids in one way or another. When I had to remove a band-aid I told my daughter it wouldn't hurt. I realized that was the wrong thing to say. In essence, I was tricking her, which over time will undermine a sense of trust in our relationship."

In order to teach your children honesty you will want to evaluate your own actions and words. You might even correct yourself occasionally to demonstrate your desire to be honest and do the right thing.

Honesty is put to the test under pressure. Sometimes that pressure is the fear of getting into trouble, or the desire to have others like you, or the strong desire to get something you want by going outside the boundaries. In each case, a strong conscience can help a child be honest even when it's difficult.

The **Bible verse** for this lesson is Colossians 3:9, "Do not lie to each other, since you have taken off your old self with its practices."

The **Power Words** that children can remember are, "I can be honest even when it's hard." The **Hero Exercise** for this lesson they've been asked to work on is to come back with an example of a time when they saw, either in themselves or in others, the pressure to be dishonest. You might help them see examples of pressure and the choice to be honest.

Talk with your children about the value of integrity in a person's life. First, it's pleasing to God. Additional benefits include a clear conscience and the building of a reputation of being trustworthy and reliable. Point these things out to your children in life and ask God for opportunities to bring these truths home in day-to-day experiences.

Blessings,

Scott Turansky

Joanne Miller

Bring on the Enemy! I'm Ready!

Preparing Your Heart to Teach Session 7

The conscience has some enemies. Those enemies are things like a desire to do the wrong thing, overactive emotions that override convictions, and erroneous beliefs such as I have the right to get revenge, or my job in life is to have fun.

In this lesson children will learn more about temptation as an enemy of the conscience. The goal is to help children see specific ways in which they might be tempted to do the wrong thing and then recognize that they can choose to do what's right.

All heroes have to face temptations. Some of those temptations come from outside, but in order for it to truly be a temptation then it must connect with something on the inside. Helping children become more aware of things that tempt them can arm them to be better prepared in those situations.

The Bible has a lot to say about temptation. Remember that your goal is to help children learn this lesson in their hearts. In addition to the scriptures taught you might want to also look at 1 Peter 5:8 and Ephesians 6:10-18, both of which have application to temptation and use metaphors of a lion and armor that children understand.

In the Bible story, reference is made to Genesis 4:7, the story of Cain being confronted by God. This is an excellent story for children and it may be worth your time and energy to develop it even more. It's one of those positive, practical applications that children can relate to.

As you continue to study the life of David and point out the characteristics of a hero, help children see that they have what it takes to be a hero and that they face many of the same challenges that heroes face. It comes down to choices and relying on the power of the Holy Spirit and the prompting of the conscience.

Supplies Needed for This Lesson

Cup Tower Supplies needed: 20-50 disposable cups per group of 3-4 children

Which Egg is Ready?
Supplies needed: Two eggs, one raw and the other hard-boiled

Responding to Temptations
Supplies needed: The two Situation Cards on page 156, four copies of each

Avoiding Temptation Game
Supplies needed: About 20 rolled-up pairs of socks and a snow saucer or large pillow

A Hero Reminder
Supplies needed: Scissors, tape, one piece of aluminum foil for each child approximately one foot square, cut into 4 strips, the Bible verse on page 157 photocopied, and 4 pennies for each child, tissue paper (optional)

Can You Discover the Trick?
Supplies needed: A broom

Don't Get Distracted
Supplies needed: Photocopy onto card stock for each child the "Don't Get Distracted" on pages 158 and 159, make the two pages front and back on the same piece of card stock, colored pens, and a stopwatch

(For Preschoolers) Resist Temptations
Supplies needed: Photocopy the Hero Color Sheet on page 160, crayons or colored pens

Session 7 ★ Bring on the Enemy! I'm Ready!

Cookies with a Special Treat Inside
Supplies needed: Make cookies according to the recipe in this lesson. Have them ready to serve the children.

Hero Field Guide
Supplies needed: The Hero Field Guides from the previous lesson and the verse from page 162, photocopied and cut for each child, glue, and crayons or markers

Can You Read This?
Supplies needed: Photocopy the Eye Chart on page 161, at least one pair of binoculars, more if you have them

Other suggested items:
• Photocopy the Parent Letter for each student.
• Be prepared to play the Conscience Song if you have the Hero Training Camp Music CD.
• Have a camera ready to take pictures.

Theme

Heroes are strong enough to resist temptation.

Power Words

I need to resist temptation in order to protect my conscience.

Theological Truth

I must do what's right even when it seems that the wrong thing might be justified.

Welcome Activity
Cup Tower

Supplies needed: 20-50 disposable cups per group of 3-4 children

Instructions: Have children work in groups of 3 or 4 to build a tower of cups. The goal is to see how high they can make the tower with the fewest cups. They can only have four cups touching the

floor or table. Take a picture of children next to their tower of cups, or be ready to take a picture just as the cup tower is falling down.

Discussion points: The key to building a tower is similar to the keys for developing one's life. It has to do with a good foundation. It's important to build one's foundation on God and a personal relationship with him. God desires to live and work in our hearts. He helps us to grow to be people of integrity. One of the ways he does that is through the conscience. God uses our consciences to remind us to stay on track with him. Building integrity happens in four areas, just like the four cups at the bottom of the tower. Take some time to remind children about the four parts of the conscience as you get ready for this lesson. They are to do what's right, deal with wrongs, be honest, and care about others. Being a hero starts in the heart.

In this lesson we'll discuss a common problem that ruins a person's internal tower. It's temptation. We are all tempted in life, but the hero knows how to resist temptation and is ready for it.

Together Time

Gather together and remind children of the Hero Training Creed. Take a few moments to help children calm down and prepare their hearts with a prayer, asking God to settle the hearts and provide

I will LISTEN with my 👀, keep my 👄 UNDER CONTROL, Do what the SAYS, knowing that becoming a HERO for God is MY GOAL.

opportunity to focus on today's training. Review the Hero Exercise that the children were assigned in the previous lesson. In our last lesson we talked about being honest under pressure. Can you tell us a time when you were able to do that in the last few days?

Hero Training Creed:

I will listen with my eyes, keep my mouth under control, do what the teacher says, knowing that becoming a hero for God is my goal.

★ ★ ★ ★ ★

Introduction
Which Egg is Ready?

Supplies needed: Two eggs, one raw and the other hard-boiled

Instructions: Show the eggs to the children and tell them the following: I have two eggs. One is raw and the other is hard-boiled. Which one is which? They look the same. Can you tell the difference? You may even let children carefully examine the eggs to see if they can figure out which one is hard-boiled.

On the outside they look the same but on the inside one is ready for the table and the other is quite a mess. Here's an easy way to tell when an egg is hard-boiled and when it is raw without opening it up. Spin the egg upright. If it is hard-boiled it will spin around and around. If it is raw, it will just wobble a bit. Take a picture of a child spinning the egg.

How it works: The liquid in the raw egg prevents the egg from spinning because the weight inside keeps shifting. The hard-boiled egg is solid on the inside making it easier to comply with the centrifugal force created by spinning.

Discussion points: Heroes are strong on the inside, not mushy. In fact, when temptations come their way, heroes are able to face them instead of giving in to them. A hero is someone who is not just strong on the outside but is strong on the inside as well. All heroes are tempted to do the wrong thing. The test is how they respond. Of course the real test of the egg is when you crack it open. When temptations come to a hero, they test what's really on the inside. Temptations always come but the Bible tells us that God never allows us to be tempted more than we can handle it.

Today we're going to see how our hero David was tempted to do the wrong thing. Will he be able to handle the temptation?

★ ★ ★ ★ ★

Bible Story
The Hero's Temptation

This Bible story is taken from 1 Samuel 25. Use the Bible and the following thoughts to teach the story and the lesson to the children. You may have to change the wording or explanations to match the developmental level of the children you're working with.

We've been studying the life of David because he was a hero. And, in fact, we see through his life that we too can be heroes. I want to tell you a story today about a time when David was tempted to do the wrong thing. It all started when David and his men, who were still running from King Saul, lived in the Desert of Maon. There wasn't much food in the desert and they often had to rely on other people in order to have enough food and water.

David and his men looked out for the local shepherds and used their skills of fighting and protecting others to help the people of the valley. As soldiers they could keep guard and protect the shepherds from wild animals and from bandits so that the shepherds wouldn't be afraid.

One of these groups of shepherds worked for Nabal. He was a greedy man, selfish, and thought mainly about himself and getting rich. In fact, his

Session 7 ★ Bring on the Enemy! I'm Ready!

name "Nabal" means fool. He truly was a foolish man because he only thought about himself.

Nabal had a lot of sheep and he hired shepherds to take care of them. When the weather warmed up they would cut the wool off and sell it so that people could make clothes. In fact, at sheep shearing time Nabal and all of the shepherds were so happy they had a party because they were going to make so much money. They had more sheep than usual because David's men had protected them from bandits and wild animals.

It was during the sheep shearing time that David and his men weren't able to find enough food, so David sent some men to Nabal to ask him for just a little bit of food. After all, David and his men had helped Nabal but he had never paid them or even thanked them for their work. So David's men came to Nabal to ask for some food.

Nabal was greedy and selfish. He not only said no to the messengers but he made fun of them and insulted them for even coming to ask. The men went away sad and reported the news to David. David was angry. This wasn't fair. Nabal was being ungrateful, selfish, and mean.

Here's where David was tempted to do the wrong thing. In fact, he told his men to get their swords because they were going to go and kill Nabal and his men. Even though it was the wrong thing to do, David was angry and so he was tempted to get revenge.

That same situation happens in our lives sometimes. Let's say that you don't get what you want and your brother is being selfish. You might feel angry and want to just take something away

or get back at him somehow. When a person gets angry they can be tempted to be mean. It's a pretty common temptation.

Even heroes get tempted sometimes to do the wrong thing. They may be tempted to be mean, or to lie, or to just do something wrong for one reason or another. Let's read on in the story and find out what happens to our hero, David.

Nabal had a wife whose name was Abigail. She was a very wise woman, and when messengers came to her and told her how Nabal had insulted David's men she quickly went into action. The Bible tells us that she lost no time in gathering food for David and she met him on the way. She rode into a ravine where she knew that David would come. When she saw him and his men she got off her donkey and bowed down before David.

David and his men stopped when they saw Abigail. She talked to David and said, "David, God has fought for you all these years. Surely he has something special planned for you. Don't do this wrong thing. If you do, you will have it on your conscience. It's not worth it. Take this food I've prepared for you and go back. Don't do this wrong thing and get revenge."

As David listened to Abigail he knew that she was right. Up to this point he had a clear conscience. He didn't need to cheat to get what he wanted. Getting revenge is being mean and if he did that he knew that he would feel guilty. Abigail was right. As David thought about it he realized that the right thing to do was accept the food from Abigail, turn back, and let God deal with Nabal. Revenge would be the wrong thing to do.

Wow. David did the right thing even when he was tempted to do wrong. It reminds me of another

Bible story. The story of Cain in the Old Testament. Cain brought the wrong sacrifice to God and so God didn't accept the sacrifice. The Bible tells us that Cain was downcast. That means that he was pouting. Show me what downcast looks like.

In the same way that Abigail confronted David, God confronted Cain. In Genesis 4:6-7 the Bible says these words, "Then the LORD said to Cain, "Why are you angry? Why is your face downcast? If you do what is right, will you not be accepted? But if you do not do what is right, sin is crouching at your door; it desires to have you, but you must master it.""

Temptation tries to get at all of us. David was a hero and he fought the temptation and did what was right. That's a battle that goes on inside the heart first. Once we win the battle inside then we can work on the outside to do what's right.

Sometimes we can feel tempted to do the wrong thing and then we tell ourselves it's okay. In David's case, he was mistreated. He was tempted to kill all of the men because they were being mean to him. Just because others are mean and do the wrong thing doesn't mean that we have the right to hurt them. We may be tempted to do that but heroes recognize the temptation and are careful to do what's right even when tempted.

Let me tell you an interesting part of the story about David. The Bible tells us that the next day Abigail told her husband Nabal all about David coming to kill him and how she gave him and his men food. Nabal was so surprised and probably afraid that he had a heart attack and within a few days died. That's an interesting end to the story. But even if Nabal hadn't died, David was still the hero because he had a clear conscience. He didn't give in to the temptation. He chose to do the right thing.

Take away: I must do what's right even when it seems that the wrong thing might be justified.

For preschoolers: This story must be simplified for preschoolers. Leave out much of the detail and emphasize the idea of temptations to do the wrong thing. Imagine some temptations that young children might face, meanness and disobedience for example. Use those as examples of opportunities to do the right thing.

Bible Verse
1 Corinthians 10:13
God is faithful; he will not let you be tempted beyond what you can bear. But when you are tempted, he will also provide a way out so that you can stand up under it.

★ ★ ★ ★ ★

Role Play
Responding to Temptations

Supplies needed: The two Situation Cards on page 156, four copies of each

Instructions: David was tempted to do the wrong thing. He may have justified it in his heart by saying that Nabal was wrong so getting back at him is what he deserved. I need some help acting out some other stories. I'd like you to work in groups of 3-4 and prepare to act out a situation for us. For a large group of children, you may have actors and an audience that participates in the discussion. For a smaller group of children, you may have the same kids act out the different stories. Be sure to take pictures of the children having fun doing drama.

Choose three or more children to act out each role play. Person #2 is the one being tempted. You can have one or more children act as Person #3, helping Person #2 do what's right. Give

children the situation cards and let them huddle for a few minutes to prepare to act out what not to do and then what they should do instead. You may want to help them as they plan.

Discussion points: What are we trying to learn from this lesson? Temptation to do what's wrong is all around us and even inside us. Heroes see temptation and look for ways to do what's right instead. Sometimes heroes also help other people do what's right just like in our story of Abigail helping David do the right thing. Being a hero often requires that we fight an internal battle before we can fight the external one.

For preschoolers: Drama is a great way to engage the heart of a preschooler. Instead of having the child plan the drama, you'll likely want to dialogue through the situation and allow children to act it out as you go.

Conscience Insight

Guilt is a healthy emotion that points toward repentance. The conscience produces guilt when one has done something wrong. God has provided a way back through confession, restitution, and reconciliation. Shame is not helpful because it focuses on inadequacy, unworthiness, and permanent failure. Shame hinders people from moving forward and removes their confidence to do what's right.

Temptation provides a challenge to the conscience. As children learn to respond well to temptation they grow stronger. Even their mistakes produce growth if they know how to handle them well.

★ ★ ★ ★ ★

Game
Avoiding Temptation Game

Supplies needed: About 20 rolled-up pairs of socks and a snow saucer or large pillow

Instructions: Have children line up on one side of the room armed with rolled pairs of socks ready to throw. Set up the other side of the room so that each corner contains a safe place, like a chair or some other barrier. Choose one child to run from one safe place to the other, trying to avoid the bombardment of socks (temptations) being thrown at him while he's out in the open. Take turns allowing several children to make the temptation run. This activity makes for some fun pictures.

Next, have one child use the snow saucer or pillow as a shield and leisurely walk from one side to the other.

Discussion points: Temptations come our way every day. What are some temptations that kids your age might face? Lying, cheating, getting revenge, obeying slowly, not completing a job, having a bad attitude, or being mean are all temptations that may come at you. A hero pays attention to the inner promptings of the Holy Spirit and the conscience and when he or she knows what needs to be done, does it instead of giving in to the temptation. A hero can deflect temptation as if he has a shield.

The Bible verse for today says that God provides a way out of temptation. But notice the rest of the verse. It says "so that you can stand up under it." Sometimes people think that they will escape by getting out of the situation, but many times you can't get out of the situation, you have to learn to be strong in it. Like having an annoying brother for example. You may wish you could get away, but God may want you to learn how to develop the inner strength to face the temptation of your brother every day.

★ ★ ★ ★ ★

Craft
A Hero Reminder

Supplies needed:
Scissors, tape, one piece of aluminum foil for each child approximately one foot square, cut into 4 strips, the Bible verse on page 157 photocopied, and 4 pennies for each child, tissue paper (optional)

God is faithful; he will not let you be tempted beyond what you can bear. But when you are tempted, he will also provide a way out so that you can stand up under it.

Instructions: Give children the aluminum foil strips with the following instructions.

Scrunch up two of the strips to make two stick-like pieces; lay them on the table to form an "X."

Twist the middle of the "X" to form a body. The top points of the "X" become the arms and the bottom two points become the legs.

Use the third piece of foil to ball up and form the head.

Use the last strip of foil to go from the back of the hero over his head and down his front to fasten the head to the body.

Bend the feet out and tape two pennies to each foot, providing stability for the hero to stand.

Attach the Bible verse between the two hands and secure with tape.

Use tissue paper to form a cape if desired (optional).

Be sure to take pictures of the children making this craft as well as posing with their little heroes.

Discussion points: Abigail reminded David of the importance of his mission in life. David was thinking more about the short-term benefits of getting revenge than the long-term benefits of avoiding temptation. You'll be able to use this hero as a reminder to avoid temptation. Every time you see it you can pray and ask God to help you resist the temptations you face. After all, God wants you to be a hero and he knows that you need reminders.

For preschoolers: Preschoolers love to take the craft home. However, it's pretty complicated for a young child to make without help. It doesn't take a long time to put each hero together, and children then like to move the arms and legs around to make it balance. Of course, preschoolers can't read the Bible verse but the message on it is a good reminder and parents may use the verse at home to further explain the concept of temptation to the children.

★ ★ ★ ★ ★

Hero Skill Building Activity
Can You Discover the Trick?

Supplies needed: A broom

Instructions: Tell the children that you want to do a trick for them and see if they can figure it out. "Your job is to try to do what I do. Can you figure out the secret?" Then take a broom, turn it upside down, clear your throat, and tap the broom on the floor to a rhythm as you say the words, "I need to resist temptation in order to protect my conscience."

Then ask, "Who would like to try it?" If no one volunteers, demonstrate it again. Be sure to clear your throat before you speak because that's the secret. It's not the broom or saying the words in a particular way. It's the clearing of the throat that you're trying to get kids to do.

Session 7 ★ Bring on the Enemy! I'm Ready!

When a child volunteers to try it, watch and see if he clears his throat first. If he does, then tell him "Yes, that's right. Who else would like to try?" If he doesn't then say, "No, that's not it, who else would like to try?"

Continue the game until everyone gets it. You may have to exaggerate the clearing of the throat if needed.

Discussion points: Heroes have the ability to see things that others don't see. When it comes to temptation they are on the lookout for it. You might see your friends start to talk in a mean way about someone else. You can see where that's leading and help them change course. When you have an assignment due and you feel like getting on the computer instead of working on your assignment, you can see it early and choose what's right. The conscience is a tool created by God that's already in your heart. It helps you by prompting you to do what's right. If you work on developing your conscience then you will often have warning of temptations before they take place. Also, the Holy Spirit lives inside of those who trust Christ. He also warns you of danger.

For preschoolers: This activity isn't for preschoolers and should be dropped out when working with young children.

Game
Don't Get Distracted

Supplies needed: Photocopy onto card stock for each child the "Don't Get Distracted" pages on pages 158 and 159, make the two pages front and back on the same piece of card stock, colored pens, and a stopwatch

Instructions: Have children choose at least six different colors of pens. Write the name of a different color than the ink used, filling up the boxes. You may need to help the children with spelling. Colors will be used more than once. For example if you use the blue pen, write red, yellow, or green. Then using the same colored pens turn the page over and color in the rectangles, each rectangle being a solid color. Colors will be used more than once.

How to play: Have one child hold the stopwatch while another child races against the clock. First see how long it takes the child to name all the rectangles that have solid colors in them. Next, turn the page over and time how long it takes for the child to say the color, not the word, in the sixteen boxes.

Discussion points: It takes more work to focus and concentrate on the boxes that contain written words and colors. It's tempting to read the word instead of say the color.

The same thing is true in life. Temptations are around us every day. Heroes have the ability to focus on what's right without getting easily distracted.

For preschoolers: This activity requires the ability to read and therefore isn't appropriate for preschoolers. Use the following activity instead.

Hero Color Sheet
(For preschoolers)
Resist Temptations

Supplies needed: Photocopy the Hero Color Sheet on page 160, crayons or colored pens

Instructions: Children can color the page while you talk about the lesson. Have them repeat the theme with you. Talk about temptations young children face and discuss what it means to resist temptation.

Focusing on the conscience is an excellent way to reach children on a deeper level. It helps children get in touch with inner promptings that God has placed inside the heart. But don't forget to talk about the Holy Spirit in a child's life. God is at work inside your child and you want to acknowledge that fact and refer to it often. In fact, your spiritual transparency is a helpful instrument for conscience development. Pray with your children, share spiritual insight, and ask your children questions about spirituality. By doing this, you're helping your children become more aware of their own hearts.

★ ★ ★ ★ ★

Snack
Cookies with a Special Treat Inside

Supplies needed: Make cookies according to the following recipe. Have them ready to serve the children. Play the Conscience Song while the children are eating (optional).

2 1/4 cups flour
3/4 cup unsweetened cocoa
1 tsp baking soda
1 cup sugar
1 cup firmly packed brown sugar
1 cup butter, softened
2 tsp vanilla
2 eggs
48 Rolo chewy caramels (unwrapped)
1 tbsp sugar

Heat the oven to 375 degrees. In a small bowl combine the flour, cocoa, and baking soda.

In a large bowl, add 1 cup sugar, brown sugar, and butter, and mix together well. Add vanilla and eggs; mix thoroughly. Add flour mixture; blend well.

With floured hands, wrap about 1 tablespoonful of dough around 1 caramel candy.

In a small bowl put the remaining sugar. Press one side of each cookie ball into the sugar. Put the cookies on an ungreased cookie sheet about 2 inches apart. Bake at 375 degrees for 7-10 minutes or until set and slightly cracked. Cool 2 minutes; remove from cookie sheets. Cool completely on wire rack.

This recipe makes 4 dozen cookies.

Session 7 ★ Bring on the Enemy! I'm Ready!

Discussion points: One of the things that makes a hero is that he is different on the inside. In the same way that these cookies have a great inside, a hero knows how to deal with the temptations that come every day. The temptations to be mean, to steal, to disobey, or to be unkind are out there all the time. Heroes know how to resist temptation because of something special on the inside.

The hero has a plan for dealing with temptation. It's not worth doing the wrong thing because it damages your heart. Use the snack time as an opportunity to review the lesson. You might ask the question, "What is the lesson we're trying to learn today?"

Hero Field Guide

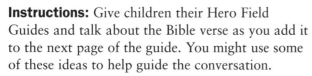

Supplies needed: The Hero Field Guides from the previous lesson and the verse from page 162, photocopied and cut for each child, glue, and crayons or markers

Instructions: Give children their Hero Field Guides and talk about the Bible verse as you add it to the next page of the guide. You might use some of these ideas to help guide the conversation.

Discussion points: God is in control and never allows us to be tempted above what we can handle. That's an encouraging point for any hero. However, if a person is bent on doing wrong then he or she will easily fall into temptation when it comes. This is a great verse to memorize because it reminds us that we always have a way to escape. It's interesting though, the last part of the verse tells us that sometimes we just need to stay in the situation and continue to do what's right.

HERO Exercise

As you practice at home look for times when temptation is present. You may not be tempted but others might be. Come back and tell us specific times when you saw a tempting situation and tell us how you handled it. For example, you might be in a situation where your mom asks you to do something. You're tempted to ignore her but you get up and do it instead. Or maybe someone hurts you and you're tempted to hurt them back. How did you handle that situation? You are a hero in training so you will experience challenges. Be sure to pay attention to your conscience and listen to the Holy Spirit in your life.

Conclusion
Can You Read This?

Supplies needed: Photocopy the Eye Chart on page 161, at least one pair of binoculars, more if you have them

Instructions: Mount the photocopied page 20 feet away and ask children to read it. They may be able to read the first line or two but then the print becomes too small to read. Ask for a volunteer who has good eyes to come and read the chart. How far down can you read it?

Now pull out the binoculars and ask for a volunteer to try to read the chart. The binoculars typically need to be adjusted. Show the children how to focus them, usually by adjusting the focusing dial in the center and spreading them so that both eyes can see. Have the child read the whole message from top to bottom. Take pictures of children with binoculars.

Discussion points: What we're trying to learn in this lesson is how heroes can see temptation in advance. They don't wait until it's right in their faces. They are quick to avoid temptation and help others do the same. You have an assignment to grow in your hero qualities. Your job is to see temptation and resist it and also look for ways to help others to resist it as well.

For preschoolers: Although preschoolers can't read, they can catch the illustration of seeing temptation coming and taking action. And, preschoolers love to figure out how binoculars work. You might create a small happy face and sad face on a paper on the wall for them to look at through the binoculars and then talk about seeing temptation before it gets to you. Be on the lookout for it.

SEEING IT THROUGH THE EYES OF A CHILD

Susan loved the binoculars and went home to see if they owned any. Dad got out his binoculars and allowed Susan to look through them. "What kinds of things are you looking for?"

"I'm looking for things that need to be done around here."

"Oh yeah?" said Dad with a surprised look on his face. "What do you see?"

"I see newspapers on the table that need to be put away. I see the tissue box turned on its side," responded Susan.

"Wow, that's great. I'll be eager to see how you fix those things that you see."

Prayer

God, I know that you love each one of these children and that you want them to be heroes in life right now. I want to ask that you would give them special glasses to see problems developing in life and that you would give them the courage to do the right thing even when they don't feel like it. Lord, thank you for the Holy Spirit that not only tells us what is right but helps us to do the right thing as well. Amen.

Session 7 ★ Bring on the Enemy! I'm Ready!

Role Play
Responding to Temptations

Situation #1
Knowing How to Respond to Meanness

Person #1: *The Mean Teaser*

You tease the other child by saying things like, "You can't play with us. You're too small. We're going to have fun without you."

Person #2: *The Victim*

You're disappointed first of all, then angry. You're tempted to get back at the mean person. You're planning your strategy for revenge.

Person #3 and others: *The Peacemakers*

You come in and give advice to the victim on how to handle the situation without getting revenge. What should the victim do with the anger? How should the victim deal with the Mean Teaser?

Situation #2
Tired, But Doing What's Right Anyway

Person #1: *The Parent*

It's clean-up day around the house. You're trying to get the kids to do some chores. Be sure to explain the value of chores and why we all need to work together around the house and the benefits for getting things done.

Person #2: *The Tired Child*

You don't feel like working. The parent leaves you alone to do a job. You look for ways to cut corners, and do the job part way so that you can go and rest and play a video game.

Person #3 and others:
The Helpers

You don't particularly like working either but you know that Mom has a lot to do, things need to get cleaned up, and if everyone works together then we'll be able to get it all done quickly. Your job is to convince the tired child to do the right thing.

Craft
A Hero Reminder

God is faithful; he will not let you be tempted beyond what you can bear. But when you are tempted, he will also provide a way out so that you can stand up under it.
I Corinthians 10:13

God is faithful; he will not let you be tempted beyond what you can bear. But when you are tempted, he will also provide a way out so that you can stand up under it.
I Corinthians 10:13

God is faithful; he will not let you be tempted beyond what you can bear. But when you are tempted, he will also provide a way out so that you can stand up under it.
I Corinthians 10:13

God is faithful; he will not let you be tempted beyond what you can bear. But when you are tempted, he will also provide a way out so that you can stand up under it.
I Corinthians 10:13

God is faithful; he will not let you be tempted beyond what you can bear. But when you are tempted, he will also provide a way out so that you can stand up under it.
I Corinthians 10:13

God is faithful; he will not let you be tempted beyond what you can bear. But when you are tempted, he will also provide a way out so that you can stand up under it.
I Corinthians 10:13

God is faithful; he will not let you be tempted beyond what you can bear. But when you are tempted, he will also provide a way out so that you can stand up under it.
I Corinthians 10:13

God is faithful; he will not let you be tempted beyond what you can bear. But when you are tempted, he will also provide a way out so that you can stand up under it.
I Corinthians 10:13

God is faithful; he will not let you be tempted beyond what you can bear. But when you are tempted, he will also provide a way out so that you can stand up under it.
I Corinthians 10:13

God is faithful; he will not let you be tempted beyond what you can bear. But when you are tempted, he will also provide a way out so that you can stand up under it.
I Corinthians 10:13

Don't Get Distracted Part 1

Instructions: Have children choose at least six different colors of pens. Write the name of a different color than the ink used, filling up the boxes.

Don't Get Distracted Part 2

Instructions: Color in the rectangles, each rectangle being a solid color. Colors will be used more than once.

HEROES

are strong enough to resist temptation.

Can You Read This?

The conscience is important.

Heroes can see temptation coming.

They take action to resist temptation.

God gives strength to resist temptation.

Heroes help others resist temptation.

I can be a hero.

God is faithful; he will not let you be tempted beyond what you can bear. But when you are tempted, he will also provide a way out so that you can stand up under it.

I Corinthians 10:13

God is faithful; he will not let you be tempted beyond what you can bear. But when you are tempted, he will also provide a way out so that you can stand up under it.

I Corinthians 10:13

God is faithful; he will not let you be tempted beyond what you can bear. But when you are tempted, he will also provide a way out so that you can stand up under it.

I Corinthians 10:13

God is faithful; he will not let you be tempted beyond what you can bear. But when you are tempted, he will also provide a way out so that you can stand up under it.

I Corinthians 10:13

NATIONAL CENTER
for BIBLICAL
Parenting

76 Hopatcong Drive, Lawrenceville, NJ 08648-4136
(800) 771-8334 or (609) 771-8002
Email: parent@biblicalparenting.org
Web: biblicalparenting.org

Heroes Have a Plan to Fight Temptation

Dear Parent,

The conscience and the Holy Spirit work together to provide inner promptings to a child. As you work with your children to help them do what's right, look for ways to encourage them to pay attention to those inner promptings.

One of the enemies of the conscience is temptation. After all, it's temptation that draws us away from doing the right thing. Children are all different. One child may face a temptation to lie or be dishonest that doesn't even bother another child. Kids face temptations to ignore instructions, hide an offense, be mean to someone else, or choose entertainment over responsibility.

As a parent, be careful to focus on what the child should do, not just what the child should avoid. For example, you may be working on telling the truth under pressure instead of just stop lying. Or maybe you're working on showing kindness instead of simply removing meanness. When parents continually emphasize the negative they miss opportunities to teach the positive. Each temptation provides an opportunity to do something right. In each situation, talk about what is the right thing to do. What heart quality are you trying to help your child develop? Focus on that positive quality and it will add a positive dimension to your parent/child interaction.

Look for ways this week to talk about temptation. The **Bible verse** for today is 1 Corinthians 10:13, "God is faithful; he will not let you be tempted beyond what you can bear. But when you are tempted, he will also provide a way out so that you can stand up under it."

Use this verse to help kids recognize temptation coming at them and have a plan for dealing with it. Not only do heroes resist temptation for themselves but they also help others resist it as well.

The **Power Words** for kids in this lesson are, "I need to resist temptation in order to protect my conscience." The **Hero Exercise** for this lesson is to be on the lookout for temptation. Teach children to pay attention to the promptings of the conscience and rely on the Holy Spirit to help them do the right thing.

Look for opportunities to partner with your child to help others overcome temptations.

Blessings,

Scott Turansky

Joanne Miller

The One Minute HERO

Preparing Your Heart to Teach Session 8

The goal of this lesson is to help children become more aware of the inner prompters to do the right thing instead of relying on parental instructions and reminders. Heroes are responsible and do what needs to be done on their own. The key is that children learn to take initiative themselves instead of waiting for prompters from parents or leaders.

One way that children can take initiative and do what's right is by learning to do more than what's expected. It doesn't take much longer to add something extra. In fact, in this lesson the idea of the One Minute Hero helps kids see that they can do a little extra in just a short time with amazing results. When asked to fold the towels, for example, they might also put them away. Or, when asked to pick up the clothes from the bathroom floor, they might clean the sink and close the cabinets too. That's doing more than what's expected.

The Bible verse, Hebrews 13:18, ties a good conscience to living in an honoring way. Honor means treating others as special, doing more than what's expected, and having a good attitude. When children learn to show honor to others, they practice skills that they'll use for the rest of their lives.

This lesson hones into a particular area where the conscience can be very practical for children, keeping their rooms neat. This one area is often a source of conflict between parents and their children. In this lesson, though, children are challenged to straighten their rooms not just to please parents, but also because it's the right thing to do.

Supplies Needed for This Lesson

One Minute Hero
Supplies needed: Photocopy the ONE MINUTE HERO Color Sheet from page 176, one for each child, crayons or markers, camera, and the Hero Song (optional)

Find the Ark Hunt
Supplies needed: Photocopy and cut out the Ark Hunt game cards on page 178. Create more game cards than the number of children in your class.

How Much Time Does It Take to Be a Hero?
Supplies needed: Camera, a stopwatch, set of adult clothes including pants, sweatshirt, hat, sunglasses, and shoes

The One Minute Check List
Supplies needed: Photocopy onto card stock the One Minute Check List door hanger on page 177 and cut one per child, crayons or markers, a hole punch, and rubber bands, one for each child

Snack Towers
Supplies needed: Square or round crackers, cheddar cheese slices, apple slices, grapes, napkins, paper plates, and a knife for cutting the cheese and fruit

Hero Field Guide
Supplies needed: The Hero Field Guides from the previous lesson and page 179, photocopied and cut for each child, glue, and crayons or markers

Session 8 ★ The One Minute Hero

Human Robot
Supplies needed: An adult assistant willing to be the robot, a piece of bread, a stick of butter, a plate, and a butter knife

Know How to Read a Map
Supplies needed: A map

Other suggested items:
- Photocopy the Parent Letter for each student.
- Be prepared to play the Hero Song if you have the Hero Training Camp Music CD.
- Have a camera ready to take pictures.

Theme

Heroes respond to needs by taking action, and often do more than what's expected.

Power Words

I look for things that need to be done and do more than what's expected.

Theological Truth

We must always listen to God who often uses the conscience to prompt us to do the right thing. Looking for ways to honor others is a good way for me to practice doing what's right.

Welcome Activity
One Minute Hero

Supplies needed: Photocopy the ONE MINUTE HERO Color Sheet from page 176, one for each child, crayons or markers, camera, and the Hero Song (optional)

Instructions: As children come in, play the Hero Song (optional) and have them sit down and color the poster of a ONE MINUTE HERO. Tell them they will learn today how it often only takes a minute to be a hero. This poster is a reminder of the lesson. Take pictures of children holding their colored posters.

Discussion points: You might use this time to review the four elements of the conscience, past lesson highlights, or talk about the assignment you gave the children in your last session together. Your students may have been part of hero opportunities but weren't aware of them. Your dialogue can help recount some of these incidents.

For preschoolers: Although young children can't read, they like to color posters like this one. In fact, they can remember the meaning of the poster even if they can't read the words.

Together Time

Gather together and remind children of the Hero Training Creed. Take a few moments to help children calm down and prepare their hearts with a prayer, asking God to settle the hearts and provide opportunity to focus on today's training. Review the Hero Exercise for the previous lesson. In our last lesson we talked about identifying temptations to do the wrong thing. Can you tell us a time when you saw a temptation in the last few days?

Hero Training Creed:
I will listen with my eyes, keep my mouth under control, do what the teacher says, knowing that becoming a hero for God is my goal.

★ ★ ★ ★ ★

Introduction
Find the Ark Hunt

Supplies needed: Photocopy and cut out the Ark Hunt game cards on page 178. Create more game cards than the number of children.

Instructions: Hide Arks in many places around the room, under several chairs, and tables, under a trashcan, on a windowsill, in a drawer, taped to a wall, some obvious and some well hidden. Have kids find the Arks and bring them back to you.

Discussion points: Heroes are people who take action. They see things that need to be done and they take care of them. We're going to see how David did that in our story today. But God had certain rules about carrying the Ark. People needed to obey those rules even if they were trying to do something good.

★ ★ ★ ★ ★

Bible Story
The Right Thing Done the Right Way

This Bible story is taken from 2 Samuel 5-7. Use the Bible and the following thoughts to teach the story and the lesson to the children. You may have to change the wording or explanations to match the developmental level of the children you're working with.

Even though David had been chosen as king, he spent several years running from Saul who was trying to capture and kill him. Then one day there was a big battle between the Israelites and the Philistines. Saul and his sons, including Jonathan, David's best friend, were killed in the battle. When David heard the news he was sad. He loved Jonathan so much.

Now with King Saul dead, it was time for a new king and who do you think would be that king? Yes, David. Finally after all those years David would be king.

David was 30 years old when he became king over Israel. The first thing he did was conquer Jerusalem, the capital city. That's where David would build his palace. David wanted to do things right. He wanted to please the Lord. He looked around for something that would honor God. Honor means to value something. David wanted to show the Lord that he valued him. What could he do?

There was a special Ark of the Covenant, a box that represented God's presence for the Israelite people. It was the Ark of the Covenant that people followed in the wilderness and the Ark of the Covenant that often led the people into battle and opened the Jordan River so that the people could walk through. David decided to bring the Ark from the priest's house where it had been stored, up to the city of Jerusalem. Then it would be a symbol that God's presence was right in the middle of the city. David wanted to honor God in this way.

God had given specific instructions about how the Ark of the Covenant should be carried. It had rings in all four corners. Two poles would go through the rings, one pole through two rings on each side. The Levites would carry the Ark by the poles but they were never allowed to touch the Ark.

David knew that the Ark was special. He wanted to do the right thing and bring the Ark up the hill to Jerusalem to honor God. So David went down to the home of the priest Abinadab and had men put the Ark on a new cart pulled by some oxen. That wasn't God's way to move the Ark but they were having a parade celebrating the movement of the Ark to Jerusalem so they decided to use the cart instead of following the instructions and using the poles.

Everything went fine for a while. People were singing and dancing as the parade moved closer to Jerusalem. Then all of a sudden one of the oxen pulling the cart stumbled; the Ark began to slip off the cart. Uzzah, one of the men walking next to the Ark, reached out to steady it so that it wouldn't fall off. As soon as he touched the Ark he dropped dead. No one was supposed to touch the Ark.

This is such an interesting story because Uzzah was trying to do something good by steadying the Ark, but he wasn't doing it God's way. David was trying to do something good too by bringing the Ark to Jerusalem but he wasn't doing it God's way.

Sometimes we have ideas about what the best way is to do something but if it isn't God's way then it won't work. If we want to do the right thing then we must learn God's ways.

The apostle Paul wrote something very interesting in the Bible. In 1 Corinthians 4:4 he wrote, "My conscience is clear, but that does not make me innocent. It is the Lord who judges me." You see, sometimes people think that if what they're doing feels right to them, then it must be right. That's not always true. David had to learn that lesson the hard way. One of his men died.

David stopped the parade, the Ark was taken to the home of Obed-Edom, a man who lived very

close by, and David went back to Jerusalem. In fact, the Bible tells us that David was afraid. He was afraid because, here he was trying to do a good thing, but God judged him and a man died.

One of the things that heroes have to deal with is fear. In fact, sometimes heroes are afraid to do the right thing and they have to overcome their fears. Sometimes fears will lead a person to do the wrong thing.

Let me tell you about a boy named Jerry. Jerry knew that stealing something from the store was the wrong thing to do, but his friends were developing a plan to sneak some candy out of the store. Jerry was afraid that if he didn't go along with the plan then his friends wouldn't like him. What do you think Jerry ought to do about his fear?

Brandi was walking with her mom at the store and saw a man drop $5 out of his pocket. Brandi knew that the right thing was to tell the man that he dropped some money but she was afraid that she might be embarrassed. What do you think Brandi ought to do about her fear?

The reality is that people often don't do what's right because they're afraid. Fear of humiliation, failure, and rejection are just a few reasons. Are there some things that you're afraid of that keep you from doing what's right? Being a hero and doing what's right require courage in the face of fears.

Fears can get in the way of doing the right thing. David was a hero. He knew that he could trust

God if he did the right thing. David heard that God was blessing the home of Obed-Edom because he was storing the Ark. For three months God was blessing that man and his family, so David sent men to his home to get the Ark and bring it to Jerusalem. This time, David told the men to move the Ark the way God had instructed. This time everything worked well. David was so excited that the Ark was now in Jerusalem.

God was pleased with David. He had a heart to serve the Lord and really wanted to do what was right. Sometimes David made mistakes. Sometimes he sinned, but God knew that David loved him and that he really wanted to do the right thing.

God sent a message to David through his prophet Nathan. God told David that he would give him a throne that would last forever. That was a very special promise. David was honored that God would give him such a special promise. David looked for ways to honor the Lord. The greatest way that David could honor God was to do the right thing.

Doing the right thing takes courage. It sometimes means that we sacrifice what we want in order to show love to someone else. It means that we take extra time to help out, care for others, or be honest. One of the ways that we can be reminded of things to do that are right is to listen to God speaking in our hearts and be sensitive to the promptings of our consciences.

Let me tell you some examples of kids who did the right thing.

James went into the living room and saw some cups and plates left over from the night before. Knowing that they didn't belong there, he carried them to the kitchen without being asked.

Jayme saw that the trashcan was full in the kitchen. Instead of just leaving it for someone

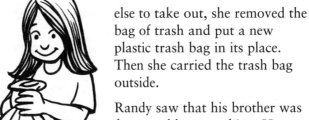

else to take out, she removed the bag of trash and put a new plastic trash bag in its place. Then she carried the trash bag outside.

Randy saw that his brother was frustrated by something. He didn't know what it was but he went into his brother's room and tried to talk to him and make him feel better. It worked and he saw his brother cheer up a bit.

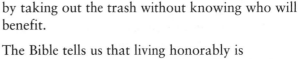

All of these situations are examples of honor. Honor means that we treat someone else as important. Sometimes we know the person that we're honoring, like when Randy cheered up his brother. Sometimes we just honor the family by putting things away or by taking out the trash without knowing who will benefit.

The Bible tells us that living honorably is prompted by the conscience. The Bible verse for today ties the two together. Hebrews 13:18 says, "Pray for us. We are sure that we have a clear conscience and desire to live honorably in every way."

This week we want to look for ways to do the right thing like King David did. But we always need to be careful to do the right thing the way God wants it done. That's why we study the Bible, to learn the ways of God and understand the things he wants us to do.

Take away: We must always listen to God who often uses the conscience to prompt us to do the right thing. Looking for ways to honor others is a good way for me to practice doing what's right.

For preschoolers: This story has a lot of pieces. If you're working with preschoolers it would be best

Session 8 ★ The One Minute Hero

to emphasize a small portion of the story. Teaching preschoolers that it's important to obey and do the right thing the right way helps them in practical terms.

Bible Verse
Hebrews 13:18

Pray for us. We are sure that we have a clear conscience and desire to live honorably in every way.

Hero Skill Building Activity
Seeing What Needs to be Done and Doing It

Supplies needed: None

Instructions: Before class begins leave several things messy or out of place. For example, put a piece of trash next to, but not in, the trashcan. Put a sign on the door crooked. Leave a coat on the floor, a drawer not pushed in, a chair turned over, and some papers on the floor in the corner.

Ask children this question, "What is an example of something that needs to be done around your house but often gets overlooked?" Trash not taken out, cups left in the living room, coats not put away. A hero sees what needs to be done and does it. There are several things in this room that aren't right. Who can tell me one that you see? Have children identify things in the room that need to be done and then have that child fix the problem. If a child points out that a wall needs to be painted or that a window is dirty, then you might appreciate the comment and go on to other things that a child might be able to fix now.

Of course, if any child has already taken care of something like turned a chair back upright or picked up the trash near the trashcan, then you can point out that the child is already exhibiting honor by seeing something that needs to be done and doing it.

Discussion points: Heroes are on the lookout for things to do that are extra. That means identifying

ways to help out, ways to serve, and taking initiative. It doesn't take much extra work. It just takes initiative to do it.

Stop and ask the children, "What is the lesson I'm trying to teach you with this activity?" Allow the children to review the concept of seeing what needs to be done and doing it without being told.

Conscience Insight
The conscience doesn't speak but it does prompt children nonetheless. It prompts by using emotions. When a child does the wrong thing, she feels guilty and is prompted to make it right. When a child sees something that needs to be done, he feels a sense of obligation.

Relying on the conscience doesn't simply mean doing what feels good. We all know that feeling good about something doesn't make it right. However, when we do the right thing, we do experience feelings of peace and satisfaction.

Game
How Much Time Does It Take to Be a Hero?

Supplies needed: Camera, a stopwatch, set of adult clothes including pants, sweatshirt, hat, sunglasses, and shoes

Instructions: This game involves racing against time. You may want to have two children working together at one time. They don't have to compete. They can work together and be in the same picture as well. When the stopwatch starts, the child puts on the clothes, glasses, and hat. He jumps onto the photo stage (a space marked out for the pictures) and gives a hero pose for the picture. When the picture snaps, the stopwatch ends the time. How much time does it take to be a hero? Keep track of the various times. Use the pictures to remind children about being a One Minute Hero. Also share the pictures with parents along with the lesson learned.

170

Discussion points:
We all know that just putting on clothes doesn't make someone a hero, but the reality is that it often doesn't take that much extra time to be a hero.

Remember that a hero is someone who does the right thing. That might take a little longer but often not too much extra time. How much time does it take to see that a trashcan is tipped over and some trash spilled out and fix that problem? Maybe a minute. How much time does it take to cheer someone up with a compliment? Maybe a minute.

In fact, let's talk about a common problem children have, keeping their rooms neat. How much time does it take to keep a room neat? Allow the children to discuss this. Some might suggest that it takes a long time to clean a room. But, if they started with a clean room it doesn't take much extra time to keep it that way.

Imagine that your room was all neat and tidy. What are some of the things that make it messy? Clothes not put away, bed not made, food or dishes in the room, toys left out, books on the floor. How long does it take to do each one of those things if you do them along the way instead of allowing them to accumulate? Just about a minute of time. How long does it take to make a bed? About a minute. How long does it take to pick up the clothes and put them in the hamper or hang them up if you do it when you take them off? Just a minute.

It only takes about a minute to be a hero. Isn't that interesting. And here's the fun part. God has placed a conscience inside of you that can help you remember to do these things. When you do a

project in your room, before you leave you'll remember, "Oh, I need to clean that up."

When you straighten up your room in this way you're learning to be responsible and to live in a clean room not just because Mom or Dad tell you to do it. You're doing it for yourself. Keeping a room clean is a great way to develop the hero quality of doing the right thing.

In our craft today, we're going to create a reminder door hanger that will help you to do the right thing.

★ ★ ★ ★ ★

Craft
The One Minute Check List

Supplies needed: Photocopy onto card stock the One Minute Check List door hanger on page 177 and cut one per child, crayons or markers, a hole punch, and rubber bands, one for each child

Instructions: Have children color the door hanger, punch a hole near the top, and fasten the rubber band through the hole.

Discussion points: Heroes rely on inner prompters to get things done. Let's imagine you're in your room and you've decided you're going to work on paying attention to your conscience. What are some of the ways your conscience might prompt you if you've decided to keep your room clean? Why do we say that it only takes a minute to be a hero?

For preschoolers: Even though preschoolers can't read, this activity is good for them. You can point out the words and what they say on the door hanger and often the children will remember what you said. The reminder of a door hanger is helpful for teaching even young children to keep their rooms neat.

Role Play
Who Can Do the Right Thing?

Supplies needed: None

Instructions: Below are two situations that are fun for children to act out. In each case, one child is the parent and another child plays the part of a child.

Situation #1
The bike in the wrong place

Who would like to be the dad in this role play? Dad's coming home from work, gets ready to drive into the driveway, and right in the middle of the driveway is a bike. And we all know whose bike that is. It's Billy's bike. I need someone to be Billy for this role play.

Now Billy, you sit here pretending that you're playing a video game. Dad, you come in the door and you're not happy. Let's see what happens. Allow children to act out the story. Typically Dad comes in ranting and raving.

Next, ask the group or Dad or Billy, "What could Dad do to try to help Billy remember to do what's right?" Have Dad role play the situation in a helpful way.

Situation #2
Mud on the floor

Who would like to be the Mom in this story? Mom comes into the kitchen and finds muddy footprints on the floor. In fact, those footprints go all the way back to the door. And, those footprints are the same size as Lisa's shoes. Mom heads out to find Lisa.

Who would like to be Lisa? OK, Lisa, you're sitting here resting after being outside playing for a while. Uh-oh. Here comes Mom. Let's watch what happens.

Ask the children, "How could this situation work out better?" Certainly Lisa could check her shoes before she comes into the house. Or, when discovering that she made a mess she could apologize and agree to clean up the mess.

How can we help Lisa remember to check her shoes? She often forgets. This isn't the first time. Mom, how could you help your daughter do the right thing and remember for herself instead of you reminding her?

Discussion points: Sometimes kids forget to do things that they are supposed to do. How do you remember to do things? Ask children how they remember to do their chores, take care of their own business, or clean up after themselves. This is often a productive brainstorming session so you might want to write down the ideas for children to see them. Part of growing up is remembering to do what you're supposed to do. The conscience is a tool that God placed within a child that prompts children to do what's right and remember to do what they are supposed to do.

Snack
Snack Towers

Supplies needed: Square or round crackers, cheddar cheese slices, apple slices, grapes, napkins, paper plates, and a knife for cutting the cheese and fruit

Instructions: Serve the sliced cheese and fruit pieces on paper plates. Give the children napkins and a few crackers. Allow the children to build small snack towers by layering the cheese and fruit slices on their crackers.

Discussion points: Use the snack time to discuss the lessons for today. You might talk about straightening bedrooms, doing what's right,

one minute hero suggestions, or the Bible story about David. Children often need a number of opportunities to look at a truth before they make it their own. Your questions, illustrations, and stories can prompt dialogue that drives the truths home.

★ ★ ★ ★ ★

Hero Field Guide

Supplies needed: The Hero Field Guides from the previous lesson and page 179, photocopied and cut for each child, glue, and crayons or markers

Instructions: Give children their Hero Field Guides and talk about the Bible verse as they add it to the last page of their guides. You might use some of these ideas to help guide the conversation.

Discussion points: Living honorably is an important part of being a hero. Honor means treating people as special, doing more than what's expected, and having a good attitude. It means looking for things that need to be done and doing them. Living honorably means doing the right thing.

★ ★ ★ ★ ★

Activity
Human Robot

Supplies needed: An adult assistant willing to be the robot, a piece of bread, a stick of butter, a plate, and a butter knife

Instructions: Tell the kids you have a robot. You can tell him exactly what to do and he does it. Point to the robot (your assistant) and tell him, "Walk over here" (pointing to the ground). The robot moves to that place. "Sit in this chair." The robot sits sideways in the chair. "Face the table." The robot turns. "Now I need someone who will give instructions to the robot to butter this piece of bread." Let one of the children be the Instructor and watch what happens. The robot should look for ways to do what the Instructor says but not exactly what the Instructor wants or means. For example, when told to put the knife in the butter, plop the knife in the middle of the butter. When told to put the butter on the bread, put the whole stick on top of the bread. This will be a funny and interactive way to teach children an important lesson.

Be sure to take pictures of the robot with the children giving instructions.

Discussion points: Why is it so frustrating to work with a robot? Because he does what you say instead of what you mean. A robot is the opposite of a hero and kids can be like either one. Robots only do what a parent says and often not what that parent means. When Mom says, "Please rake the leaves out of the flower bed," and you just leave them on the grass, that's like being a robot. When Dad asks

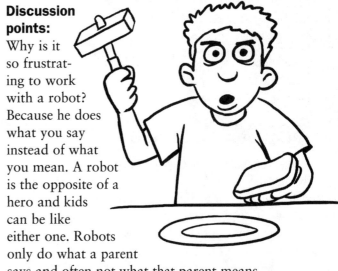

you to turn down the music and you turn it down one notch, that's being a robot because you know he wants you to turn it way down.

A hero not only does what the words say, but a hero also does what someone expects, and even more than what's expected. That's a big difference.

Children often rely on parents for initiative. Parents wish that their children would see what needs to be done and do it on their own. Since that's the goal then it's important to parent in a way that moves children in that direction. You might say, "Son, I'd like you to sit down for a moment and think of a couple of ways to add to family life today. What can you do that is helpful or encouraging?" Or, when it's time to leave, instead of saying, "Get your backpack," you might say, "Since we're leaving in five minutes, what do you think you need to have to walk out the door?" Stepping back and requiring children to think about what needs to happen will train them to start taking initiative on their own instead of waiting for parental initiative to get them moving.

★ ★ ★ ★ ★

HERO Exercise

Look for ways to strengthen your conscience. Remember that the conscience has four parts. Can anyone tell us what those four parts are? Do what's right, deal with wrongs, be honest, and care about others. As we work on developing those areas in our lives, we take on hero-like qualities. God prepares us in the small things to be strong on the inside. Today you can take home your Hero Field Guide that you've been working on for a long time. Take your guide home and

look over it often. Read the Bible verses and the Power Words to remind yourself of ways that you can be a hero. If you continue to practice, you'll be surprised at the ways God will use you as a hero now and in the future.

★ ★ ★ ★ ★

Conclusion
Know How to Read a Map

Supplies needed: A map

Instructions: Here's a map. Using this map I can tell how to get from our town here to this town over here. I just follow the path. Point out your current location on the map and then locate something else on the map. Show the path that will take you there. You could also make your own map or print one from the Internet.

Discussion points: God has a path he wants each of us to follow. In fact, it's a path inside your heart. He wants you to grow into a hero. Of course, God's Word is the greatest road map for our lives.

We all need a road map for growing more mature. In our lesson today we tried to focus on some specific ways to build maturity by doing the right thing. It's important to look for things that need to be done and do them. Some kids think that the only thing to do in life is to play. They play video games, play on the computer, play outside, play with their friends, and when it comes time to do a little work it's as if they're surprised. It doesn't take a lot of work to be a hero, but it does take some.

In the next few days spend time thinking about what's really important about life. Is it just playing or are you ready to become a hero? You don't have to be an adult to be a hero. It can start right now.

SEEING IT THROUGH THE EYES OF A CHILD

Jack left Hero Training Camp determined to develop some new skills and become a hero. He decided that his room was a great place to start. Mom had been making him clean his room for years but he always did it for her. Now he decided he would try to keep it neat for himself. At first it was hard. He was tired, or interested in another activity, or he just didn't feel like it, but it wasn't long before he trained himself to take the one extra minute and straighten things up. It worked. His room stayed neat most of the time. Of course Mom was pleased and even surprised that Jack could do this all by himself.

On Sunday, Mom heard some of the ladies talking. They needed someone to help out at the church barbeque to oversee the tables and serve some food. Mom recommended Jack. "But we need someone who is neat and responsible to do this job."

Mom replied, "Jack is very responsible. He keeps his own room clean and he's quite organized himself."

The ladies were pleased with the suggestion and decided to give Jack the job. Mom went home and told Jack and his eyes grew big. "That would be fun!"

Jack had a great time at the barbeque and enjoyed his role on the serving team. Others saw Jack there and were amazed that such a young guy could be so responsible. Jack was developing a reputation with others. Who knows what else he'll be invited to do. Where did this all start for Jack? At Hero Training Camp and then practicing keeping his room neat.

★ ★ ★ ★ ★

Prayer

Lord, thank you for doing so much extra for us. We know that you created the stars and the flowers and the animals for our enjoyment. Thank you. We're also grateful that you sent Jesus to be our Savior. Please teach us how to add extra to life too. I pray for each of these students that you would show them how to be heroes on the inside. We know that you are watching our hearts and that you want us to be heroes. Teach us how to do that and remind us with your Holy Spirit. Thank you. Amen.

One Minute Check List

Photocopied by permission from the National Center for Biblical Parenting

Session 8 ★ The One Minute Hero

Ark Hunt Game Cards

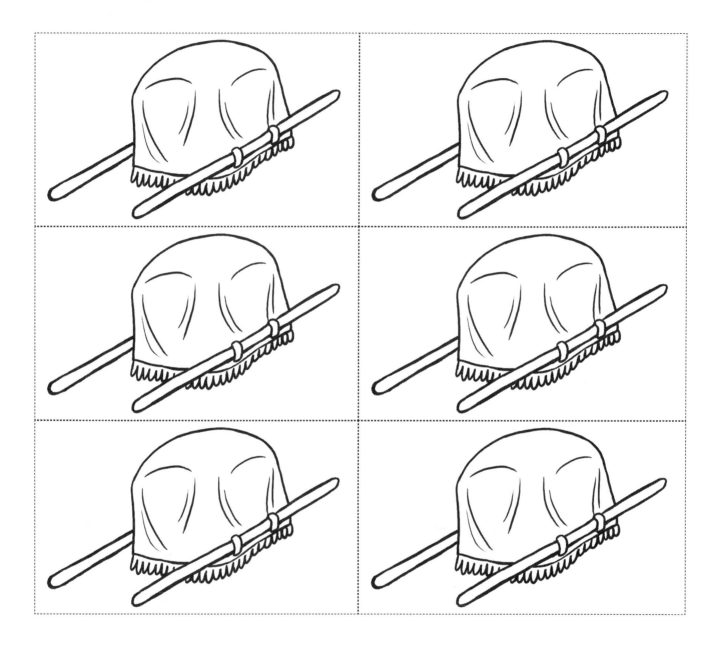

Photocopied by permission from the National Center for Biblical Parenting

Pray for us.
We are sure
that we
have a clear
conscience
and desire to
live honorably
in every way.

Hebrews 13:18

Pray for us.
We are sure
that we
have a clear
conscience
and desire to
live honorably
in every way.

Hebrews 13:18

Pray for us.
We are sure
that we
have a clear
conscience
and desire to
live honorably
in every way.

Hebrews 13:18

Pray for us.
We are sure
that we
have a clear
conscience
and desire to
live honorably
in every way.

Hebrews 13:18

76 Hopatcong Drive, Lawrenceville, NJ 08648-4136
(800) 771-8334 or (609) 771-8002
Email: parent@biblicalparenting.org
Web: biblicalparenting.org

Being a Hero Often Only Takes an Extra Minute

Dear Parent,

One of the things that characterize heroes is that they do the right thing. Sometimes that's a morally right decision but often it's simply being responsible and doing what needs to be done.

In fact, heroes have this ability to see what needs to be done and do it. You might encourage your child this week by sharing things that you see need to be done and how you did them. Those may be things around the house like recognizing that the trashcan is dirty and washing it out, or seeing that we're low on milk and buying more from the store.

The **Bible verse** for this lesson comes from Hebrews 13:18. "Pray for us. We are sure that we have a clear conscience and desire to live honorably in every way." Notice how the word conscience and living honorably are tied together. Honor means "to value" and can be defined as treating people as special, doing more than what's expected, and having a good attitude. In practical terms this means adding to family life by doing extra or by simply being responsible.

The **Power Words** for this lesson are, "I look for things that need to be done and do more than what's expected."

One of the ways that children can practice being responsible is in the care of their bedrooms. We talked about how if you keep your room neat as you go, it doesn't really take that much more time. We called it the One Minute Hero. Your child made a poster and door hanger to display in the bedroom as a reminder. Just a minute spent here or there can keep things neat. Just one minute can encourage someone else or add the extra that makes a person a hero.

Of course, if your child's room is a disaster, this might be a good time to get it to a place where a child could practice neatness. Your help in getting the room to a manageable level may be just the encouragement your child needs. That may mean getting rid of some of the extra stuff or using some storage boxes.

Look for ways to encourage your child but be careful of praise that just focuses on externals. Instead of saying, "I'm pleased that you cleaned your room," you might say, "I can tell you're enjoying being neat." The parenting focus needs to move from parental (external) prompters to internal prompters. Look for ways to affirm what God is doing inside your child. In doing so, you'll be helping your child become more sensitive to internal prompters.

Blessings,

Scott Turansky   Joanne Miller

Photocopy the following pages.

It's nice if you photocopy the first page on card stock.

Then fold and staple them like a book.

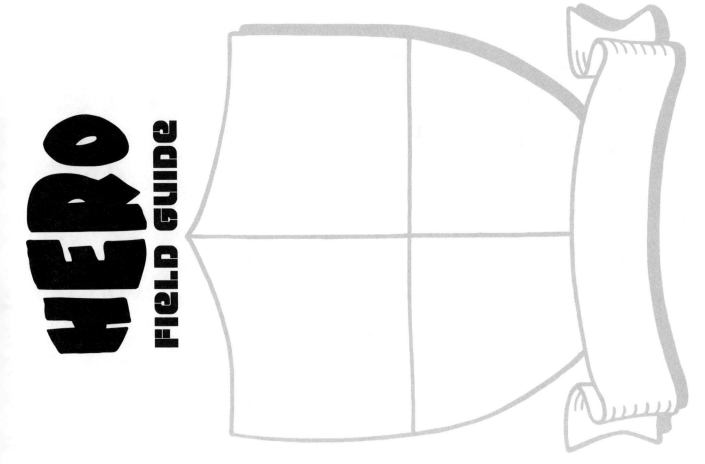

HERO
FIELD GUIDE

Welcome to **HERO TRAINING CAMP**

Four things characterize a hero.

1. Do what's right

2. Deal with wrongs

3. Be honest

4. Care about others

In this training program you will learn how to develop

skills in all of those areas. It takes practice to be a

hero. So work hard and be ready for a great training

time. You never know what challenges will come your

way as a hero so you have to be ready. We're here to

help you.

Work hard!

Session 1

I AM EAGER TO DO WHAT'S RIGHT.

Session 8

I LOOK FOR THINGS THAT NEED TO BE DONE AND DO MORE THAN WHAT'S EXPECTED.

7

Session 7

I NEED TO RESIST TEMPTATION IN ORDER TO PROTECT MY CONSCIENCE.

Session 2

2

PROBLEMS, INTERRUPTIONS, AND CHALLENGES ARE MY MISSION.

3

Session 3

I WILL DEVELOP CONVICTIONS BASED ON GOD'S WORD.

Session 6

I CAN BE HONEST EVEN WHEN IT'S HARD.

6

5

Session 5

I KNOW THE POWER OF ADMITTING WHEN I'M WRONG AND ASKING FOR FORGIVENESS.

Session 4

4

I'M ALWAYS ON THE LOOKOUT TO HELP OTHERS.

Free
EMAIL PARENTING Tips

Receive guidance and inspiration a couple of times a week in your inbox.

Free Parenting Tips

Get practical suggestions to help you relate better to your kids and help your kids change their hearts, not just their behavior.

The tips are gleaned from the live seminars, books, and articles of Dr. Scott Turansky and Joanne Miller, RN, BSN. Here's what parents are saying about these short words of encouragement.

"We have a three-year-old and an eight-year-old, and so many tips apply to both. It's exciting for me when God delivers a tip on something we're struggling with and I'm able to share it with my husband. It get's conversation started and good things happen."

—mom of two, Wichita, KS

"Just wanted to let you know what a blessing your parenting tips have been to me and the others I share them with. I make copies of them to pass around and also save them in a file. They truly help me and other parents learn practical and biblical principles of parenting."

—children's pastor, San Diego, CA

"These tips are very helpful and actually seem to come at a time when I need them. I have three teenagers ages 16, 14, and 13, so I always need help with something."

—mom of three, Ewing, NJ

To receive Free Email Parenting Tips sign up online at www.biblicalparenting.org or fill out the form at the left and mail it in. Also available in Spanish. Visit www.padresefectivos.org.

Sign up for free email parenting tips now. (You can remove yourself from the list at any time.) Your email address will not be shared or sold to others.

_____
Name

_____
Address

_____
City

_____
State   Zip

_____
Phone number with area code

_____
Email address

NATIONAL CENTER for BIBLICAL *Parenting*

76 Hopatcong Drive
Lawrenceville, NJ 08648-4136
Phone: (800) 771-8334
Email: parent@biblicalparenting.org
Web: www.biblicalparenting.org

Run Another Children's Program Emphasizing Family Issues

Reaching children can often lead to change in family life. Whether you run the children's program during a parenting event or run it independently, children learn ways to contribute to family life.

We offer two more choices for a children's program that emphasize character development and strong family relationships.

Kids Honor Club

Using the concept of honor, children explore ways they can add energy to family life. Complete with Bible stories, crafts, activities, and games, these thirteen lessons will help children ages 3-12 think differently about how they relate in their families. This curriculum was written to complement the parent training material, **Say Goodbye to Whining, Complaining, and Bad Attitudes, in You and Your Kids.**

■ $29.95

Treasure Hunters

Hidden within the common experiences of family life are treasures every child needs. Learning the value of correction, how to accept no as an answer, and the importance of a good attitude are important now but also for the future. Each of these eight lessons will help children ages 3-12 learn how to be more effective in their families. This curriculum was written to complement the parent training material, **Parenting is Heart Work.**

■ $24.95

Everyday Parents **CAN** Raise Extraordinary Kids!

Video series by
Dr. Scott Turansky and Joanne Miller, RN, BSN

Parents learn to help their children be internally motivated instead of relying on parental prompters in four areas: Doing what's right, Dealing with wrongs, Being honest, and Caring about others. Join Dr. Turansky and Mrs. Miller as they teach parents about the biblical concept of the conscience and encourage its development.

**8 Packed Sessions • • • 21 Parenting Strategies
Rooted in Theology • • • Amazingly Practical
You'll see change in 30 days whether your child is 3 or 18**

- Learn how a heart-based approach differs from behavior modification
- Understand the difference between the conscience and the Holy Spirit – and how to take advantage of both in parenting
- Identify your own convictions and learn how to teach them to your kids
- Teach children to take initiative and be responsible
- Apply these principles to parenting children of any age
- Understand Attention Deficit Disorder and provide kids with hope
- Using five tools, develop a plan for change in 30 days
- Coach children to handle their emotions
- Help kids respond better to correction
- Develop honesty in practical ways

When you *focus* **on the conscience,** *good things* **happen!**

Parenting is Heart **WORK**

Do VBS Differently this Year...
Train the Parents Too!

VBS

Get your kids ready for the training of a lifetime!

Five days of fun-filled activities, children rotate from Station to Station, learning how to be heroes in daily life. Support materials are available to help publicize the event, train the leaders, teach the preschoolers, and get the kids involved.

Request a promotional CD today by emailing parent@biblicalparenting.org.

For Children Ages 3-12

● ● ● ● ● **OR** ● ● ● ● ●

Family**VBS** Plus

FOR KIDS

Everyday Parents **CAN** Raise
Extraordinary Kids!
Video Series

FOR PARENTS

Include the parents so that families are learning together. Part of the time parents work with kids. The other part parents and children learn separately. Everyone learns about the biblical concept of the conscience to motivate kids to do what's right, deal with wrongs, be honest, and care about others.

Learn more at biblicalparenting.org